HEARTACHE TO HEALING

NAVIGATING GRIEF AND FINDING PEACE

LLOYD C. DAVIS

You Will Never Walk Alone

Heartache to Healing, Navigating Grief and Finding Peace
© Copyright <<2024>> Lloyd C Davis

Heartache to Healing, Navigating Grief, and Finding Peace

ISBN: 979-8-89109-749-0 (paperback)
ISBN: 979-8-89109-752-0 (ebook)
ISBN: 979-8-89109-753-7 (hardcover)

Library of Congress Control Number (number pending)

Unless otherwise noted, Scripture quotations are taken from the King James Version Bible, public domain.

Credits
Published by Selfpublishing.com
Cover design by Selfpublishing.com
Edited by Staci Mauney, Prestige Prose, LLC, prestigeprose.com

For more information, email: lloydc.davis@gmail.com
Visit my website: https://www.lloydcdavis.com/

Get Your Free Gift

Your Own Grief Journal

A Grief Journal is a great place to record your thoughts and feelings about your deceased loved one. It is wonderful to record your most personal memories as you navigate your own journey to find healing and peace.

Download your free Grief Journal at:
https://lloydcdavis.com/free-gift/

In the pages of a grief journal, we find solace,
a safe haven for our pain, and a path toward healing.
—Unknown

DEDICATION

I want to dedicate this book to my beloved late wives,
Cheryl, and Robin, and to my late wonderful son,
Daniel, who have returned to their heavenly home.

My love for them is boundless, unconditional, and eternal.

I miss them very much and look forward to the glorious
day when I am once again reunited with them.

CONTENTS

PREFACE

Grief is personal. *Everyone grieves differently.* There is no one-size-fits-all all. It doesn't just go away if we ignore it. We don't "get over" our grief—we learn to manage it. We can work through our own grief and discover how to live with it. Our grief never ends, but it can get less acute and less painful. We don't move on from our grief. We can move FORWARD in a positive way while embracing our grief.

As we progress along our path to healing, the intensity of our grief can diminish. We can get to where it is bearable, and eventually, our journey can bring us to find healing and peace. To become at peace with our grief is possible, as is the clarity and calmness that comes with being at peace with our grief. I am not telling you how to grieve or that you should do exactly what I did on my own journey toward healing. This book provides you, the reader, with my story and how I worked through my grief and found healing and peace. Hopefully, I can assist you, and give you ideas that you can use on your own journey toward healing.

When I write about my grief, I am not just mourning the loss of a loved one, but I am also mourning the loss of our earthly life together.

INTRODUCTION

My Transformational Journey Through Love, Sweat, and Tears

Grief /grēf/

Noun/Meaning: Deep sorrow, especially that caused by someone's death.

This is a book written not by a psychiatrist or grief counselor or with a clinical or scientific approach, but this book is written by someone who has lived and is living through the devastating loss of a loved one. I am approaching the subject of loss from a purely HUMAN approach. There have been many books written about loss from a purely scientific or clinical viewpoint.

This book is written by someone who knows what it is like to actually have their feelings and their reason ripped right out of them when they lose someone close to them. I have read books on bereavement and loss, and they can be helpful. They can assist the mind in understanding loss. They can give you general steps for overcoming grief. But many of them do nothing for the heart or the soul.

I want this book to reach you, my readers, in a personal way. By reading about my journey, I hope you can relate to what I went through—relate to what I felt and what I experienced. So yeah, I am there—I have experienced the deep ache of sorrow and the overwhelming weight of grief that accompanies the profound loss of someone dear to your heart. It is my prayer that you will be able to find something in this book that will assist you in your grief, to assist you in your journey.

When someone close to us passes on, we feel physical pain—the physical need to see them, to look into their eyes, to caress their face. The longing to touch them, and to clasp their hand in ours; to embrace them, to kiss them on the forehead, and to hold them. There is also emotional and spiritual pain. Our spirit has a longing as much as our body does if not more. When we lose someone close and dear to us, we feel the pain down in our souls. Perhaps that is why it is so difficult to move forward. We don't "move on" after we lose a loved one. *I will not use that phrase as an option for dealing with our grief in this book.* Because, for me, that is never an option. Our loved ones will always be with us. They are with us daily in our thoughts, our pictures, the songs we hear, the smells we smell, and the things we see, and the places we go. All these things bring back memories of them. Our loved ones are truly always with us. Moving forward is very difficult, and sometimes it seems impossible for us to live through our grief.

The purpose of my writing this book is hopefully to provide assistance to anyone who is struggling with the loss of a loved one and to be able to help you find healing. It is my desire that through my experiences, what I have learned through my journey, and how I dealt with and am dealing with my loss, I can assist you in finding the healing you need.

God can give us the strength and inspiration to live through the loss of a loved one to find healing and peace. Heaven knows I have leaned on God many times throughout my journey. When I speak of peace, I am speaking of personal solace. The word *peace* can mean a lot of things to different people. What I am writing about in this book is the personal peace that I have found and that I feel within my grief after the loss of my loved ones. Finding peace begins with finding the healing we desperately want and need after our loss. The title of my book has a deep, personal meaning to me—working through our grief, and our heartache, to find healing and peace by navigating our own journey after the loss of our loved ones.

It was the deaths of my two beautiful wives Cheryl and Robin, and my brave son Daniel, that set my feet upon this journey to find healing and peace. It was on this journey that a wondrous transformation has taken place within me. As I sought healing, my heart began to mend, gently piecing itself back together. Through this process, my mind found a newfound clarity concerning the loss of my loved ones and their physical absence from my life. Along the way, my spirit was uplifted and revitalized, gaining strength from my experiences and the lessons that I learned while working through my grief. The path I undertook to find healing and peace has led me to a place of profound growth and renewal, filling my heart with fulfillment and love.

My love for them has been strengthened greatly. I will always mourn them, but my grief has been tempered, and the acute, devastating pain that I felt is no longer debilitating or running my life. I have found joy in the knowledge that I will be reunited with them again. This has brought my soul to be at peace with my grief.

Please know that I am not being boastful here; I am very grateful and humbled for the lessons that I have learned and for the experiences that I have had throughout my journey.

The healing that I found didn't come overnight, but over time, and with a lot of patience it did. My path of working through my grief was not easy; it was a difficult journey to get to where I am now. It took a lot of prayer and hard work to find healing and peace. My journey took a lot of introspection and soul-searching. It took **love, sweat, and tears**. Yeah, I am humbled and very grateful that my efforts have brought me the healing that I needed and so desired. That is what I wish for you to achieve. It is well worth it. The reward for your hard work will be incredibly profound, humbling, and life-changing. It is truly transformational.

This journey that I have traveled has been a long road, beginning with the death of my first wife, Cheryl.

Grief doesn't go away or cease when we have worked through it and have found healing and peace. I still mourn for and miss them very much. They will always be a part of me, along with our memories. My life with them has made me who I am today. As we move forward, we can feel strengthened and edified.

As I worked through my grief, I came to the realization through my experiences that we never "move on" or "get over" the loss of a loved one. We can simply learn to find a way to move forward and live with our loss, in light and love.

Following their passing, as they each returned to their heavenly home at different times, my journey of growth and progress continued, propelled by the steps I took to work through my grief.

Wow, it is a reachable goal, and it can happen. I want to say that with God's help, all is possible, Especially the healing of your broken heart. I hope you enjoy this book. I pray that you can find something valuable in it to assist you on your own journey.

CHAPTER 1

Cheryl

My Original Inspiration for Writing This Book

The reality is that you will grieve forever.
You will not "get over" the loss of a loved one; you
will learn to live with it. You will heal, and you will
rebuild yourself around the loss you have suffered. You
will be whole again, but you will never be the same.
Nor should you be the same, nor would you want to.
—*Elisabeth Kübler-Ross*

*I sat in my car with my children, getting ready to drive home from
the cemetery after my second wife Robin's funeral. With tears in my
eyes, I thought,* Not Again.

Thirty-six Years Earlier
Cheryl

I looked into her beautiful big brown eyes, captivated by the
radiance of her warm smile, as we traveled hand in hand on our
journey to Seattle. With a boundless grin, my heart surged with

an overwhelming blend of love and joy. I knew that I wanted her to be my eternal companion, to cherish and to hold. This was the first vacation that I ever took with Cheryl, and it was one of the greatest times of my life—driving, talking, laughing, and reveling in each other's love. I was living a dream, traveling with the woman that I love so very much, to a city that I also love.

> *Life is a journey that must be traveled no matter*
> *how bad the roads and accommodations.*
> —*Oliver Goldsmith*

On August 12, 1995, my first wife, Cheryl, passed away, just a day before her thirty-first birthday. She took her own life. Cheryl was suffering from a brain tumor. She also had hypothyroidism and was bipolar, as well as suffering from depression.

The day that I married Cheryl was one of the happiest and most wonderful days of my life. That day we united our lives as one, and she became Cheryl Davis. I was struck by her beauty, not just her outward appearance, but even more so by the magnificence of her inner beauty. Cheryl truly is a beautiful woman.

Through our marriage, I learned so much from Cheryl. We traveled our journey of life's ups and downs together, with our three boys Derrick, Daniel, and Samuel. Along the way we went through a major medical crisis with our youngest son, Samuel. We spent a lot of time with different doctors to find out what the issue was. As a result, Cheryl's health suffered. During this ordeal, Cheryl and I went through the wringer emotionally, physically, and spiritually.

This journey to find out what was wrong with our son really took its toll on Cheryl. She experienced bouts of depression and didn't eat properly and had significant weight loss. We found out that she had a brain tumor, that led to her suffering from migraines. Her depression along with her bipolar disorder and her weakened physical condition led her to her final moments on earth when she took her own life. In life, Cheryl was my greatest teacher and one of the bravest women I have ever known.

In the midst of Cheryl's journey through challenging times with her mental well-being, there were moments when she grappled with irrational and misguided impulses. Regrettably, she felt that our shared path as a married couple should reach its end. It was a painful process that spanned many months, during which I poured my heart into conversations aimed at showing her the value of our continued marriage. Even amid these trials, our love for each other remained. It was too painful for Cheryl to see how her slipping grasp on reality was affecting me and the boys. She believed that parting ways would serve the best interests of both us and our beloved children. She confided in me about the pain she felt while acknowledging the hurt she unintentionally caused us.

After several months, with a heavy heart, I agreed to the painful choice of divorce. Ultimately, her struggles with mental health became an unbearable burden for her, leading to her taking her own life. I have spent much time reflecting on this. I know now that I could have handled things differently. At the time I was scared and confused from watching Cheryl suffer through her psychological and physical decline. There were times when she was lucid, and I could get a glimpse of the wonderful woman that I married.

Our separation before she passed away did not prevent us from holding onto our love, and we have reconciled our relationship. It is my belief that marriage continues after death, and Cheryl and I are bound together for eternity.

I can remember vividly when I had to sit down with our boys and tell them that their mom was gone and would not be with us anymore, as well as how it felt to tell them. As a parent, it is the most difficult thing I've ever had to do, to look in my children's eyes and tell them that their mom will not be coming home. I guess it was fortunate in a way that my eldest son, Derrick, who has Down syndrome, really had a limited understanding. But he did feel it when his mom was no longer there with him physically. He knew and understood that she had died; he hurt, and he cried.

My youngest son, Samuel, was just two years old; he doesn't really remember his mom. But when Cheryl passed, he did feel her absence. Her death hit our son Daniel very hard. He loved his mom so much and was affected very much by her death.

I took the boys into a room and sat them down and gave them the horrible news. My stomach was twisting, and my heart ached for our children, as well as for myself. It took all the strength I could muster to get the words out. My parents were there for our support, which I will always be grateful for. My mom held our youngest son, Samuel. I looked into my two oldest sons' eyes and saw their tears; I gave them a hug and did what I could to comfort them, but it just seemed, well, not enough. That whole day spun around in my mind. To anyone who is reading this book, I am sure you can totally relate to this—relate to how it feels to break the news. To break the news of the death of someone you all care a great deal about. This experience is very emotional and sobering; it is heartbreaking.

The task of telling our boys about their mom was difficult for me— Cheryl loves her boys so very much; she absolutely adores them. Having this thought in my mind as I prepared for this most daunting task, brought up so many emotions. The task of having to actually sit down and tell our children that their mom had died brought up so many things. It brought up memories and emotions while I was preparing to deliver the bad news. Thoughts about what I would say. Thoughts about how they would take the news, and thoughts about what I would do after I told them.

My mind raced and spun to come up with the words I would say. Should I just say, "Boys, your mom is dead"? Should I remind them of how much their mom loves them, then tell them? Should I go into a lecture about God's plan for us to live as families forever as a buildup, and go through a Sunday School lesson to prolong the inevitable? My mind spun with these thoughts and so many others. I thought about what words I should use so that they would understand. I wondered about how I would answer their questions. A whirlwind swirled in my mind, and my proneness to overthink things was not helping at all.

My parents offered to do it, but no, I was their father, and I knew that I should, and I would take care of it. I said a much-needed prayer for guidance.

As I prepared for this moment, a flood of cherished memories washed over me. Our family is bound together in laughter and love. The unforgettable vacations we shared, like our magical journey to Disneyland and SeaWorld. It was a trip that forever imprinted itself on our hearts. I can still hear the boys' infectious laughter as they rode the attractions, while Cheryl carried the precious gift of life within her; she was pregnant with our youngest son, Samuel. We captured countless moments, from snapshots by the grand castle to comical photos that I took of strangers' feet when they asked me to take a photograph of their family. Those memories held the essence of our joy, Daniel's chuckles, and Cheryl's knowing smile. Yet Disneyland brought a brief wave of panic when we momentarily lost sight of Derrick, a chilling glimpse into every parent's darkest fear.

After a short time, we discovered him engrossed in conversation with Cinderella, a heartwarming relief. And who could forget the awe-inspiring Electric Parade? Our boys reveled in its enchantment. SeaWorld, too, etched itself deeply in my recollection. The boys' excitement soared as they encountered sharks, petted stingrays, and marveled at dolphins. I meticulously positioned us in the orca's "splash zone." But it was Daniel who found wonder in the majestic presence of the killer whales, their grace and power leaving us breathless. These memories intertwined within me as I wrestled with the weight of delivering the devastating news.

The warmth of our vacations and the laughter from our local Utah trips brought a smile to my face. These memories, along with the silent prayers in my heart, gave me the assistance and the solace that I needed. This, along with my love for my children and my deceased wife, became my pillar of strength as I mustered the courage to reveal the truth to our children.

The guidance I received from my Heavenly Father helped me decide how to tell our boys about their mother and gave me the clarity I needed. I sat the boys down, with my mom holding our youngest. It was an emotional moment, especially for me. We were quiet for what seemed an eternity. After almost a minute of silence and tears, their questions came. Awkwardly, I answered the best I could, not because of my lack of knowledge, but because I was also sad and in pain and emotional. My parents assisted with answering their questions as well. I was definitely glad they were there with me, when I gave the boys the fateful news.

The emotions that I felt during this time were all over the map— sadness, anger, anxiety, fear, and confusion to name but a few. My emotions swirled while I prepared myself to talk to the boys. I had never experienced anything like this before. I had to do what I needed to do and tell the boys that their mom had passed away. This filled me with heartache and sadness, of course, because the boys had just lost their mother, along with my own sadness about losing Cheryl. But I was in fear of not only what I was going to say to them but also unsure of how I would handle their reactions and questions to this dreadful news.

Fearful of what was next . . . what do we do now . . . how am I going to raise three boys alone? I knew that my family would assist us, but I was now a single father.

Yikes! Yeaowzabunga, damn, and %$@#&! I really had no idea of how to go forward, being a single parent, along with trying to deal with my grief and supporting our boys while they were grieving for their mother. I am sure that those of you who have lost a spouse can understand what this feels like—the pressure, responsibility, and fear of being a single parent after your loss. Along with the fear came anxiety and confusion. Anxiety with the fear of what's next, as well as with not knowing what to expect or anticipate. I was experiencing anxiety on steroids.

Not knowing what I was going to do now, I was insecure about whether I was up to the task. About whether I could really do it, alone. A multitude of emotions, including fear, sadness, frustration, and confusion, resulted in many sleepless nights. I'm sure many of you can understand and relate to this.

I also felt anger—anger with others whom I felt played a role in Cheryl's mental deterioration, which led her to the taking of her own life. I indulged in the "blame game." I was angry with myself and for the role that I had played in contributing to her declining mental state. I kept feeling that I could have done more to prevent it. I felt that there was plenty of blame to go around. I decided that the anger that I was feeling and the blame I was pointing around was not serving anything or any purpose, or me. I realized it was not healthy, and I decided to let it go. Blame was pointless now. What I could do was learn from my mistakes, move forward, and put my trust in the Lord.

I frequently approached my Heavenly Father in prayer for what I needed, for myself and for the boys. Through prayer, I received what I was searching for, whether it was inspiration, comfort, or strength. I am a strong believer in the power of prayer. Our Heavenly Father's love was continually expressed to me, through the many blessings that I received and continue to receive from him throughout my journey of working through my grief. For this, I am eternally grateful.

It's been my experience, that when we lose a loved one, we need to "press on," and not let our grief swallow us up. Always move forward. At times we struggle, at times we stumble. That is okay—that is normal. We all face challenges and moments when we feel frustrated, and we struggle, from time to time. It's important that we don't be too hard on ourselves when we do.

Then we dig deep and get up and dust ourselves off. Reach out to whatever higher power we believe in—reach out to our Creator. Because you see, when we lose a loved one, it is bigger than just us. Their death and the pain that goes along with it ripples out beyond ourselves and our own personal pain. It affects others as well, who also feel the pain of our loss.

We need—I needed—to heal my broken heart and find peace. To truly be there and assist my children. I am not saying here that, *Yeah, I did it, so you can do it too.* I am really writing about the importance not just to us but also to others whom we love. That we continue to move forward on our journey toward healing and peace. Through love, healing is possible. Families are eternal.

Cheryl's death became the primary reason and inspiration for why I started writing this book.

When we lose someone we love, we must learn not to live without them, but to live with the love they left behind.
—Unknown

CHAPTER 2

My Spiritual Quest

Don't Blame God

The spiritual journey is not a solo endeavor.
It is the unification of the heart, mind,
and soul with the divine.
—Gabrielle Bernstein

While I was grieving the loss of my wife Cheryl, there was a particular song that I listened to a lot. This song really brought Cheryl to my mind and to my spirit. It reminded me of her strength and her love of God. I would think of her when I listened to it, bringing me comfort and stirring my emotions. The song is "The Ravine" by the rock group Ace of Base.

After Cheryl's passing, I went on what I call a spiritual quest or spiritual journey if you will. I felt spiritually lost and was looking for answers and ideas as well as theories on the spiritual aspects of death. I knew that death was the separation of the spirit from the mortal body. I had theological knowledge that there is life after death, and that I would be with her once again—the basics of what we call the plan of salvation. A basic part of the plan of salvation is what happens to us after we die: Where do we go when we die? Is there a heaven? What happens when we get there? Will our loved ones be there waiting for us? I knew the answers to these questions, and having this knowledge of the *plan of salvation* comforted me.

But I wanted to know more. I delved into religious reference materials. In particular, the Holy Scriptures. I also read the writings of inspired men and women. Reading these materials added to my previous knowledge and was useful when dealing with knowing what happens to us after we die. My years of study and learning led me to have a solid knowledge of our life after death. I was just looking further into theories about God's plan of salvation. Because of my religious upbringing, I knew the basic answers to these questions. But I had a burning desire to understand and know more. I feel that many of you might be able to relate to this.

After Cheryl died, I was hurting, and I was hungry to gain more knowledge. Was it truly her time? What was the purpose of her death? Was her sudden and tragic death a coincidence that just happened or a part of a bigger plan? I was trying to reconcile in my mind all of this and the fact that I do not believe in coincidences. My mind was grasping to know, to understand. God must have a bigger plan for us, and I wanted to know more about what that plan was. This led me to my search for further knowledge and understanding.

During this time, after Cheryl's death, I was curious, and I wanted to learn more. The pain that was gripping my heart drove my desire to understand. I prayed for inspiration, strength, and comfort throughout my journey to find healing and peace. My Heavenly Father is always an incredible source of guidance and comfort for me.

I delved into additional resources for information. One source I really enjoyed looking into was Native American beliefs, traditions, and practices. I studied about the Great Spirit, Mother Earth, Father Sky and other fascinating teachings and verbal stories passed down through generations among Native Americans. I also took part in sweat lodges, fire walks, and my own spirit walk. These Native American practices and traditions were beneficial to me and to my emotional and spiritual state.

Sweat lodges were beneficial to me and provided me with much healing. This practice mended parts of me emotionally. I often think of sweat lodges as sweating out our pain and whatever needs to be released from our soul. The purging of emotional impurities, if you will. I released emotions and feelings of guilt that I harbored. It was to me, in part, a process of physical and spiritual purification.

The spirit walk is very personal to me. It allowed me to travel with my spirit toward a calming and an awakening of myself. It was enlightening and allowed me to focus inward. To me a spirit walk is just that—you journey with your spirit in search of knowledge and understanding. I did that. It is also where you can find your spirit animal. That was incredible and very cool to me.

I also studied Celtic culture and even parts of the Druid beliefs. I've always been drawn to their community, and I love their music, poetry, and literature. I listen to a lot of Celtic music and just "be still." It relaxes me, brings me comfort, and calms my mind. It helps me center myself.

The Druids have a strong connection to nature—to all her wonder, strength, and beauty. Nature has such a strong spiritual component to her; it is truly humbling and amazing.

The Druids' love for nature and her creatures is serene to me. We are here, on earth, and we are part of her natural beauty.

I did search outside of the traditional and usual teachings of my faith during my spiritual quest. This simply expanded the knowledge that I already had. It helped me create a strong tapestry of understanding and beliefs that aided me throughout my journey to find healing and peace.

My faith gives me solace and strength. It is such a huge comfort to know that we do go on after our death—that there is, after all, life after death. And that in death it doesn't end there. Knowing that I will be with my deceased loved ones after I pass on is empowering and comforting. That knowledge really put my mind at rest and guided my healing. It is also wonderful to know that families are forever. We can be an eternal family together for eternity. That is truly awesome and humbling, for you can indeed be with your loved ones again.

As another part of my spiritual journey at this time in my life, I attended a local self-awareness training. It was very enlightening and assisted me in taking an honest look at myself, really for the first time in my life. I gained a lot of spiritual growth and self-awareness during my training. I also volunteered frequently at this training, where I took on roles in staffing and coaching, as well as being their ropes course coordinator for a brief time. I feel the many hours that I spent there were very valuable for me. It was on a similar self-awareness and team-building ropes course, that I did my first fire walk.

Fire walks are strengthening and taught me much about focusing, particularly the focusing of my spirit. When you're doing a fire walk, people often say it's mind over matter—don't focus on the hot coals that can scorch your feet, but rather focus on the end goal, which is getting across the HOT coals with bare feet. But I think of it differently; I look at it as spirit over mind, letting your spirit guide you over the heat and embers of life to joy and freedom.

This "spiritual quest" that I went on may not be for everybody. I am sharing this with you as one of the aspects that assisted me while working through my grief. This helped me greatly throughout my journey, and the comments and interpretations that I have written about in this book were gleaned from my experiences and study.

As I wrote about earlier in this chapter, after Cheryl's death, I felt spiritually lost—confused and did not really know what to make of losing someone that I love so dearly. I knew what happens to us after we die. But when death hits so close to home, as I'm sure you understand, life takes on a whole new meaning. Losing a loved one is the most painful experience anyone can go through on this earth.

Life looks completely different through the eyes of those who have lost a loved one, and I would wish this on no one. When you lose someone close to you, everything looks different. Our lives suddenly change into a whole new reality, and *nothing is ever the same again.* I'm sure many of you understand exactly what I'm saying: *everything changes.* All the "whys" and "how comes" explode to the surface of our minds, and we look for answers to these questions, while also looking to regain some stability in our lives. This is a delicate path that we now have to walk, because like I wrote before, how we respond to our grief, affects more than just ourselves.

There is an aspect of anger—anger that I have seen in others—that is too important not to write about here in this chapter. The anger that I'm writing about here is the anger that someone has toward God after the loss of their loved one.

I can understand why someone who is grieving does this. Through talking with others who blamed God, when they lose someone close to them, it is my belief that this is mostly out of fear and pain. Fear naturally arises in response to such terrible loss. But this can be a tool of the adversary to cause us more pain and suffering, to cause us to turn away from our Heavenly Father. It can be used to distract us. To put it plainly, it really makes no sense at all to be angry with our Creator for the death of a loved one. For He is our Heavenly Father, our staunchest supporter, and our ultimate fan. We are His children, and His love for us is boundless.

Choosing to be angry at God for your loss keeps you from finding healing. Such strong anger with our Heavenly Father does not aid us in seeking forgiveness and clarity.

If you're angry with Him please look deep inside yourself and reach out to Him for the clarity, strength, and comfort that you need. For he is waiting. I understand the frustration of being left behind. But the journey to healing is about love and the life that you and your deceased loved one shared.

After each of my loved ones passed, I did not choose to be angry with God. I know that some people I have talked to have chosen to direct their anger toward Him, as a response to their loss. As for me, I refused to go there, I refused to blame God for my loved one's death. It just was not in me to do that. I know it's because of my faith and my love for my Heavenly Father that I chose not to be angry with or blame Him. I want to clarify that I don't believe that my faith is stronger than anyone else's. I'm simply sharing that my faith holds great significance in my life and played a pivotal role in why I didn't hold God responsible, and it genuinely saddens me when I see others placing blame on Him.

Love is the way to find healing and peace: That is where our focus needs to be while we are grieving, please choose light and love. I know that through my experiences, healing is not found in anger. Again, *there is no healing found in anger.*

Seek His guidance, for God is the embodiment of love, He is the source of all truth. His love for you is immeasurable, and He yearns to alleviate your pain. God desires to mend your broken heart, so if any remnants of anger toward Him linger due to your loss, I implore you to release it and approach Him in prayer, seeking His forgiveness. Please understand that I hold no judgment of you; my sole intention is to support you. Personally, I, too, had to humble myself and reach out to my Heavenly Father, to ask for His forgiveness.

It is crucial to embrace humility, transcend our self-centered thoughts, and let go of our egos. Holding on to our faith and avoiding spiritual despair, as I once experienced, is of utmost importance. If you find yourself having lost faith or are struggling with it due to the departure of your loved one, I sincerely hope that you take the necessary steps to rediscover and strengthen your faith. It is my personal experience that having trust in our Heavenly Father is the way forward to finding healing and peace.

It is through our unwavering belief in God and His perfect love that we can attain forgiveness, healing, and clarity. Whatever method resonates with you, remember that God's love is the path that leads us forward, for we should not be harboring anger or assigning blame to God for our loss. Instead, choose to love Him wholeheartedly and beseech His assistance. You can accept His love and blessings on your journey toward healing and ultimately finding peace in your grief.

Yeah, I get it—I have been there. I have lost loved ones and felt the incredibly devastating pain of that loss. I know what and how you are feeling, I truly understand.

I hope you can learn from my experiences and what I have learned through my journey of working through my grief. Being angry at God and blaming him is not the path forward. It is not the solution or the way to find healing. As I have written, the way to finding healing and peace is through love.

Love God and accept the boundless love that he has for you. All you need to do is ask.

God's love is a flame that burns eternally, lighting our path and warming our hearts even in the darkest times.
—*Unknown*

CHAPTER 3

Embracing My Emotions

They Were Telling Me Something

I will not say, do not weep, for not all tears are an evil.
—Gandalf, The Lord of the Rings, Return of the King

Another step that I took, was that I needed to acknowledge and embrace my emotions. They were telling me something— they were communicating to me about my emotional state and where I stood in my journey through my grief; if I would only listen. For instance, if we have feelings of anger or guilt, these are emotions that need to be dealt with if we want to be able to move forward and find healing. When we have a strong desire to address our grief and to attain happiness, we need to strive to connect with our emotions and identify areas that need attention. By doing so, they can lead us to healing and the resolution of the issues that these emotions illuminate.

I understand that there are those, including myself, who have experienced incredible loss and struggled to accept and confront their feelings. It can be challenging to acknowledge and process our feelings, it takes being willing to face the emotions that are necessary to heal.

It was easier for me to not face them. To divert my attention elsewhere. To focus on anything except what I was feeling. In my opinion, the most misleading phrase I can think of is "I am fine." When people asked me, "How are you doing?" I would say "I'm fine." Wow, not only was I deceiving others, but I was also deceiving myself. Acknowledging and facing my emotions was so painful. Avoidance was much easier.

To avoid facing my emotions and what I was feeling, I told myself "I had to be strong for the boys." In that moment, I felt deeply the weight of responsibility resting on my shoulders— The responsibility of taking care of the boys, as well as giving them much-needed support. Our boys had just lost their mother. They are dear to me, and witnessing their pain only added to my own. We tried to have some semblance of a "normal" life, which was not easy, as I'm sure some of you can understand.

Our boys were young at eleven, seven, and two years old. I missed Cheryl very much, that I can tell you. But I kept myself busy with the boys and with my business, so I wouldn't have to focus on my grief. I also made some mistakes that were a result of trying to bury my emotions in dating a lot of women, looking for validation and to escape the loneliness. This "flesh binge," as I call it, did not help me with moving forward after her passing. It just diverted my attention from where it needed to be. At the time, being a young widower with young children brought me a lot of attention from single women. Yup, I did indulge.

Not dealing with my emotions was not healthy for me, either spiritually or emotionally. Simply stated, I was masking my pain by seeking attention from women, which took my focus away from my boys.

My parents were an enormous assistance to me and the boys. and spent a lot of time watching and helping me with them. My family also provided a lot of moral support and strength for us. They were there when I needed them and they showed up huge for us. I don't know how I would have gone through all of this without my family and their support.

While mourning my late wife, I put on a good front. I thought I was doing well and had put my wife's death "behind me." Nothing could have been further from the truth—I was lying to myself. After Cheryl passed away, I was just "sleepwalking" through my grief for some time. I was slowly walking through a fog—it was a fog of confusion that I created for myself. I knew how I was supposed to feel—all the emotions that I had read or heard about. But they were all just words to me. I didn't know how to deal with my emotions. I didn't know what real grief was or felt like until then. I did not want to face the gut-wrenching excruciating pain that comes along with losing someone you love dearly. It hurt; my heart was broken, and I just wanted it to all go away.

This was the first time that a close family member of mine had passed away. Cheryl was my first wife and the mother of my boys. This was all new to me. I'm sure that many of you can relate to this. I scooted along, working my business, and raising our boys. In time, I no longer wanted to feel that terrible pain and anguish anymore. I wanted to face it; I wanted to deal with it. The reality was that I didn't know how—this was all new to me. I didn't know how to deal with my grief or even if I should. I didn't want to investigate what my emotions were telling me, because this frightened me. I did not want to feel it, because I was afraid of what I might find if I did. Looking down that "rabbit hole" scared the crap out of me. I was afraid that if I did, I would see something that I did not like, or want to acknowledge. Then I'd have to deal with it. This kind of fear really sucks! The fear that keeps you from facing your emotions and dealing with your grief.

There are so many opinions out there when it comes to loss and how to deal with it. I was often told to just get back to work, and that working hard was the answer to deal with my loss. Well, being self-employed does make that a necessity. Working hard and running my business was something I needed to do to provide for my family. Hard work is vital to life and raising a family. But it is my belief that using it as an avoidance is not a healthy thing. I understand that the concept of immersing oneself in hard work as a solution to grief is often suggested, but from my personal experience, I have come to realize that it is just a way to avoid facing our pain. Using work as a method to evade confronting our emotions and the valuable messages they convey can lead our focus away from where it is truly required. Focusing on our Grief, Ourselves, and our Loved Ones.

It is essential to acknowledge and honor our feelings, allowing them to guide us in the healing process. Only by truly engaging with our emotions can we find genuine solace and growth amid our sorrow.

I found that avoidance and replacing my grief with superficial and temporary distractions were not working. Eventually, I listened to what my emotions were telling me. I now had some direction to navigate through my grief. With the assistance of my Heavenly Father through prayer, reading inspirational writings, and counsel from family and friends, I started focusing on working through my grief. I created a memorial for Cheryl on a virtual memorial website.[1] Writing this memorial about her did assist me a lot. Sharing my feelings with others about Cheryl on her memorial page was comforting and really began my healing.

I was finally ready to begin my journey toward healing, forgiveness, and ultimately peace. I discovered that grief comes in waves or sometimes tsunamis. I had days where I was just going throughout my day, and suddenly something would trigger a memory. Then along with the memories came the waves of emotions, sometimes even a tidal wave of emotions, that flooded through me. It could be sadness and a longing for them, or it could be happiness and joy.

While living with our grief, we have days when we are calm and good. We also have days that are turbulent—when the pain and sadness are more than we can bear, days when emotions and memories can overwhelm us, when we just want to curl up and stop feeling. When I am having one of those difficult days and when my emotions are high, I allow myself to embrace and feel them. I feel that listening to them, and however we wish to experience them. serves as a way for us to attune ourselves to the messages of our hearts.

Some days are good, and you are dealing with your grief, and you feel all right. Then you hear a song, watch a movie or TV show, or see or smell something that reminds you of your deceased loved one. In that instance their memory floods back to you, with a wave of emotion and love. Sometimes you laugh, sometimes you cry, and sometimes you do both. You see, it is my experience and belief that we never truly "get over" our grief. We learn to live with it, to where it no longer holds us captive. Yet, as time passes, we begin to grasp the subtle shift within us as we work through our grief toward healing. Our grief, though never completely vanishing, transforms into a gentler ache, a bittersweet reminder of the profound connection we share with our deceased loved one. It becomes more manageable, allowing us to navigate the labyrinth of emotions with newfound resilience. Each day, we face our grief head-on, drawing strength from the memories we hold dear.

It may be difficult to say that it gets easier, for the void left by our loved ones can never be fully filled. But we begin to find solace in the rhythm of life once more. As I worked through my grief, I found myself feeling this way. I noticed the pain becoming less acute. Throughout my journey of working through my grief, the intense pain that held me and my heart captive no longer engulfed me. My heart was truly healing.

As we continue this journey of healing, we learn to embrace the beauty and purpose that remain, while honoring our loved ones in the process. To be frank and truthful about this, through my experiences in dealing with my own grief, I have found that living with our grief after our loss is anything but easy. As I am sure you definitely know. So, you see, I don't like to use the word *easy* when dealing with and living with our grief. Avoidance is easy; taking the steps toward healing requires great strength, love, and humility to embark on the courageous journey through our grief. To find the healing that we need, and that our broken heart so desires, is a pursuit well deserving of the dedication and emotional effort it demands.

During my journey of working through my grief, I continued to acknowledge my emotions, embracing them, and listening to them. You see, I have found that as we work through our grief, our emotions change and can morph into different and even new ones. Emotions that can make you say, "What the heck am I feeling?" If I was confused by what I was feeling, I relied on my Heavenly Father for clarity.

As my sadness lessened, the fear for our future was still there. I had some anxiety. Like where do we go from here? What would be best for me and our kids? I experienced a wave of intertwining and even conflicting emotions while dealing with my grief and worrying about the future. These emotions served me well. It made me more cautious and thoughtful about the decisions I was making and would make. Sometimes I just had to slow down, take a breath, and prayerfully seek guidance from my Heavenly Father. Because it was just more than me that I needed to think about, I had my family to consider. Which made me much more cautious when making decisions moving forward.

Throughout my journey, I know what it is to avoid and not acknowledge my emotions. I also know the importance of accepting and embracing them—and being in tune with what they are telling me. Because true healing and peace come through acceptance, forgiveness, and love. I have found that there is NO growth or healing in denial. I hope and pray that you can learn from me and my experiences, and that you may know the importance of accepting and embracing your emotions. They are telling you something—listen to them. They can guide you.

We can travel this journey alongside our deceased loved ones and be comforted and inspired by them, allowing their light to guide us forward with renewed strength and a profound appreciation for them, and the precious bond we share with them. For they are our driving force as we navigate our path toward healing and peace.

I have found healing and I have learned many lessons while navigating my journey. Thankfully I am indeed stronger and wiser because of this.

> *Acceptance doesn't mean resignation; it means*
> *understanding that something is what it is and*
> *that there's got to be a way through it.*
> *—Michael J. Fox*

CHAPTER 4

Creating Virtual Memorials

Putting My Loved Ones in a Sacred and Honored Place in My Heart

There are special people in our lives who never leave us,
even after they are gone.
—D. Morgan

As I navigated my journey, it was vital to me that I put my loved ones in a sacred and honored place in my heart, a personal space for just them and me. I know that they will always be with me, but I felt a need and a desire to put them in a special place in my heart—a place for each and every one of them. This is a holy space for me to cherish their memories as well as our love. This is very important and special to me; it is personal—a beautiful, peaceful place in my heart and soul for them that is off-limits to anyone else. It is OUR sacred space.

I'm sure that many of you can appreciate the importance of holding your loved ones in this special place in your heart—a place the world cannot touch, being only for you, and your deceased loved ones, where you can honor them always.

I found that even though I was very willing to share the story of my loved ones and how they died, I always seemed to be holding a part of our story back. It wasn't because I was hiding something, or that I didn't want to share the details of my loved one's passing with others. I'm always open about how they died and what led to their death. But there came a time when I realized why I was guarded when sharing about them— it was because I felt I needed to be respectful and honor them and myself as well.

Certain aspects of my relationships with my departed loved ones are deeply personal, meant only for me to cherish and hold onto in my heart. This allows me to honor those memories and feelings that belong solely to me and them. This is a hallowed, sacred space that we share together with God. It is a place of gratitude as well, for I am eternally grateful to my Heavenly Father for bringing them into my life.

I invite you to do the same as you work through your own grief. Honor your deceased loved one. Put them in your heart, in a space meant just for you and them. A holy place where you can honor them, in gratitude to God for bringing them into your life. A space of openness and love, that you share only with them.

This was so very important for me, not only because they are my inspiration for this book, but because they, and my relationship with them, are sacred to me; we are an eternal family. Their stories, and how I worked through my grief, are the primary focus of what I am sharing in this book: my journey toward healing, forgiveness, and peace.

The life that we shared is filled with so many wonderful memories—with lessons that we learned together, and from each other. Positive, and happy memories, as well as painful, and sad memories, are all a part of the rich tapestry that we wove together. I really feel that on your own journey toward healing and finding peace, it is important you remember everything, both positive and negative, that you shared with them. It all—everything—shaped your relationship with them. In my experience, I found that only focusing on positive or happy memories, smiles, and giggles would not completely serve me while I worked through my grief if I wanted to find true healing.

To truly move forward with complete clarity, we need to remember the negative memories as well as the positive ones. Otherwise, to me, it is a sugar-coated journey, and not the complete voyage. If we take a glossed-over, honey-covered path, it can fail to give us the essential clarity required for genuine healing. Throughout my journey, I realized that I needed to look at and face everything—all aspects of our life on earth together. It took courage and humility for me to do this. But darn it, I did just that; I did face both the positive and the beautiful, as well as those moments that were challenging, and times of sorrow during our earthly lives together. This brought me the true healing that I was longing for.

I am grateful to my Heavenly Father for giving me the courage and the guidance that I needed. You see, I desired to have true clarity while dealing with my grief, and this cannot come if we are not willing to be totally honest with ourselves. Man, that was hard for me to do. At times self-reflection was painful for me. But wow, with Heavenly Father's divine assistance, I got there. I found genuine clarity that allowed me to move forward with authenticity and integrity. This served me well, and for that, I am very grateful.

If we want to have true healing and clarity that will serve us as well as our loved ones, we need to be completely open with ourselves throughout our journey. We need to be willing to look at all aspects of our lives that we shared with them, warts and all, if we want to find real healing and if we want to truly find peace. Remembering the tough times and how we worked through them with your deceased loved one is vital. This is where we can arrive at lasting forgiveness. You see, it is through addressing the most challenging moments that we shared with our deceased loved ones, that forgiveness can be found. Something beautiful can arise from facing our most painful moments—healing.

Walking down this path of moving forward and working through our grief needs to be an all-in effort if we desire the transformation we are in search of. Literally, we will get out of it what we put into it. That sounds like a cliché, but it is my experience that this is true. When I was not "fully in" during my journey, I got mediocre results. At first, I was not willing to be fully honest with myself, thinking that I was giving it my all, when truthfully, I wasn't. I was choosing the coward's way out, and my results showed my effort. Well, in that case, my lack of effort. Gratefully, my attitude changed, and I chose to go all in while working through my grief. As a result of this decision, I have found genuine healing and peace.

If you "lean in" fully and really work through your grief with love and truth, you will get results that are indeed transformational. Your relationship with your loved ones who have passed on will strengthen and grow. This I know of firsthand. Love is always the key factor in our journey. It binds us together and strengthens us. Go for it—dedicate yourself to your journey of finding healing and peace. Lean all the way in and be willing to be vulnerable as well as truly honest with yourself. This is part of the way forward to healing, and your reward can be absolutely liberating.

As a part of navigating through my grief, I have created a virtual memorial for each of my deceased loved ones, Cheryl,[1] Daniel,[2] and Robin.[3] When I created the memorial for Cheryl in 1995, they didn't have a lot of options for content; just the basic posting about your loved one and your memories. With Robin's and Daniel's pages, I was able to add music, photos, and all kinds of nice content.

The links to their memorials can be found in the references section of this book. I would be honored if you wanted to look at them, and possibly get some ideas for you to create a virtual memorial for your own deceased loved ones. I have found this to be truly cathartic and healing. Expressing how much I love and care for them publicly is to me, a special way for me to honor them.

When I wrote and created them for Cheryl, Daniel, and Robin, I wrote about them and how much I miss them, as well as my feelings for them. With Robin's and Daniel's, I added more content as time went on, as I still do. Most times I add pictures along with my postings on social media, particularly Facebook.

This is a way for me to honor my deceased loved ones. These memorials include many of the social media postings that I wrote in honor of them, along with the music that I chose, picture collages of them, and other thoughtful items. These thoughtful memorials are a lovely and great place to honor your loved ones who have passed away. It is very cathartic to share with others, your public statement of how much you love, cherish, and honor them.

Their virtual memorials are out there for all to read on the web forever, or until the internet dies, is nationalized by the government, or AI takes over everything.

If you would like to create a virtual memorial for your deceased loved one, the virtual memorial website can be found at https://www.virtual-memorials.com/. [4]

Keeping my loved ones "alive" in my memory and in my heart is all a part of my moving forward. My great love for them made it important for me to protect and cherish their memories. Our love for each other has sustained me throughout my journey and gave me important clarity that I needed to move forward and not sit still and wallow in self-pity.

The memory of our loved ones becomes a
treasure that brings us strength and comfort.
—Unknown

CHAPTER 5

Daniel

Choosing to Move "Forward" in a Positive Way

No parent should have to bury their child.
—*King Théoden,* The Lord of the Rings:
The Two Towers

*"Dad, my head really hurts," my son Daniel said to me while we were having dinner and watching a movie together as a family. "And it's not working right. I just need to go to my room and lie down for a while." Several minutes later my cell phone rang; it was Daniel calling. When I answered the call, I heard Daniel's muffled voice speaking very incoherently and mumbling. I couldn't understand a word he was saying. It DIDN'T sound like him. He didn't sound right. I thought he must be tired. I asked him, "Daniel, what's wrong?" Then a few seconds later, he hung up. I sat confused and perplexed, and then I heard, "**BANG!**" It sounded like a firework, and it came from the basement. I ran downstairs, and a dreadful horror filled my eyes.*

On February 26, 2017, our son Daniel passed away. He took his own life in his room, in the basement of our home.

Daniel had been on seizure medication for twelve years; he began taking his medication at age seventeen. The meds Daniel was taking, Dilantin and Lamictal, are meant to be taken under strict doctor's supervision. He was not to deviate from his prescribed dosage without his doctor's instruction.

A couple of weeks before his death, Daniel had altered how he took his medication without telling us or consulting his physician. This was indeed very serious, and it led to a drastic reduction in his cognitive reasoning. This was the major contributing factor that affected his mental capabilities or mental state on that fateful, sad day. He was not in complete charge of his mind.

After hearing the bang, I ran down into his room, and I smelled what I thought was something burning—like Daniel had possibly burned something in his room. It also smelled like a firecracker had been lit off in his room; oh shit, it smelled like sulfur.

Then as I entered his room, my heart dropped out of my chest. There was Daniel, lying on the floor in a pool of blood. He had shot himself through his temple. I ran to him, grabbed him, and cradled him in my lap. I was completely in shock; everything in my head swirled. There I sat on the floor of my son Daniel's bedroom, holding him and weeping uncontrollably. My son, my beautiful son, lay there dead with his bleeding head in my lap. I could feel my heart breaking with the intense pain and sadness of that awful moment. I was living a parent's worst nightmare. It didn't feel real; this just could not have happened. Please, God, wake me up from this horrible dream, I thought. *My flowing tears expressed my deep anguish.*

After what seemed an eternity to me, through my sobbing I yelled to my wife Robin to call 911 because Daniel had just shot himself. Robin and my youngest son Samuel came running down the stairs and saw us both there. Me, sitting, sobbing, holding my beautiful son Daniel in my arms; lifeless. That day was one of the darkest days of my life. I was living a true bona fide nightmare, playing out in real-time. "Oh, Father! Why?" I cried out in pain to my Heavenly Father.

Daniel, my buddy, a great kid, a great man. Always thinking of others. Daniel has such a beautiful soul. A very dear friend of mine said at his funeral that "Daniel was too good for this world." My father has said to me many times that Daniel had no guile, that he had a pure heart with no malice toward anyone.

Now, there I sat, looking at his face, his beautiful pale face. While scenes of activity went on around me. Robin calling 911, Samuel standing there in disbelief, and Elizabeth and Derrick were upstairs where they were told to stay. My mind felt like it would explode, and my heart was breaking. I was in a *daze*, until Robin brought me back to that horrible reality with her loving embrace. Once again, the death of a loved one, had found its way back into my life.

After Daniel's death, my journey of working through my grief toward healing began, AGAIN. I now had a brand new, painful chapter to add. Crap, here we go again. Well, I had dealt with the death of a loved one before. But that did not make this any easier; it just compounded it. The pain that I felt was intense, and my heart had been broken once more. In my heart, I wasn't supposed to outlive my son.

Thankfully, with God's help, I dealt with the death of my son in a positive way, and I have found healing and peace and have been able to move forward. I honor my late son, Daniel, and his life on this earth—it has been one of the highest honors of my life, to be his father and watch him grow into the great man he became, to witness the great moments of his life as well as the times when he stumbled, and to applaud him, and to help him up when he needed me to. Our Heavenly Father gave him to us to watch over and to raise. For this, I am eternally grateful. I so look forward to the day when we will be reunited once again.

When a loved one passes away, it has been my experience, that we really have three options in how we deal with their death: we can choose to take the dark path, which is the negative path; we can choose the path of light or the positive path; or we can choose the path of indifference and completely ignore or stuff our emotions and feelings.

The dark path is the negative reaction to our loved one passing on. Whereas the light path is choosing to move forward in a positive way, and the indifferent path is choosing neither—it is just existing in nothingness and feeling no emotion. The cold path.

The course we ultimately choose to take holds the key to our destination. From my own personal journey, I have discovered that the positive path is the one that truly leads us toward healing, forgiveness, and peace. Conversely, the negative or dark path tends to breed anger, frustration, and unhappiness. Another path that may emerge is that of indifference, where we become cold and unfeeling in the face of losing a loved one and refusing to acknowledge our emotions, a big component of this path is denial. This path entails merely existing without truly processing the depth of our feelings, and embracing a detached reaction to our loss. My experiences have shown me that neither the dark nor the indifferent paths are a healthy way to deal with one's grief.

The path I perceive as dark seems to lead toward destruction. In my personal journey, I have come to realize that embracing negativity is detrimental to our spiritual and mental well-being. It can even have adverse effects on our physical health. On the other hand, when we choose the path of positivity—the path of light—we propel ourselves forward with love and a positive mindset. Choosing to proceed in a positive way brings forgiveness and understanding through love. We can use the love and affection that we hold for those we have lost as a beacon to guide us along our journey to finding healing and peace.

The death of a loved one is excruciatingly painful. Our separation from them through their death is probably the most painful experience a person will ever have to go through in their lifetime. The vacancy and gaping hole that it leaves in our life is at times too painful to endure. When we lose a loved one, we are faced with the decision of how we will respond and deal with our acute loss—either with debilitating anger or with love, or not at all. That choice is entirely up to us, and whether we really want to find true healing. The path of light is always open to us with God's assistance.

I know people who, after the death of a loved one, chose to go dark. Based on what they have told me, this was driven by anger, fear, and blame. It is my belief that choosing anger as a driving emotion is destructive to a person's spirit. It affects one's state of mind. Now, at first, it can seem natural to us to feel angry. But it is how we deal with that anger that defines us and guides us on our journey when dealing with our loss.

As for me, I was angry at first, especially after the death of my son. His death was so sudden. I was angry at myself, then at the doctors and Daniel for his "self-medicating" and changing how he took his meds. The anger that I felt toward Daniel quickly dissipated as I let it go. Being angry at my son didn't make any sense or serve me at all. The anger that I felt was brief because I understood the circumstances of why he had taken his own life, and because I loved him so much. It didn't serve any purpose to be angry at my deceased son. And being angry at the doctors was illogical. I didn't feel that my anger toward them was justified at all—I was just looking for someone to blame. I was confused and in pain because I had just lost my son. *No parent should have to bury their child.* I was sad, and I was hurting.

I decided that being angry with myself was not what I should be feeling as well, and it was providing no assistance to me while dealing with my grief. Being angry at myself was counterproductive and pointless. It did not serve me or my family at all. In my experience, anger is a reaction to our fear. So, I chose to feel love instead. Love for my son, my family, and myself. That was the way forward for me when navigating through my grief. This path allowed me to choose life.

Being angry is a human reaction. But to hold on to that anger does not serve anyone, nor does it have any constructive purpose. It serves the opposite; it serves as a powerful opening for the adversary to take us into a place of darkness. The dark path is not healthy for the mind, spirit, or body. It leads to negative thoughts—thoughts that can be destructive and judgmental.

From my experiences, the emotional well-being of someone who chooses anger can be delicate and fragile. I know that for myself, this was true, even though I did my best to hide it. I was looking for something or someone to blame and to vent my anger toward. My anger clouded my thoughts and obscured my judgment, leading me to believe my actions were justified.

It was like my mind was engulfed in a fog and was clouded by my despair and pain, it really impaired my discernment. Anger can easily find its way into our thoughts and feelings.

But when we decide to let go of the anger, this is where healing can truly happen. As I have written, shortly after I chose to let go of the anger and I chose love (with God's assistance), I chose to travel the path of light. And I am so grateful that I did.

At times, anger can unexpectedly surface as a way to escape confronting the truths we wish to avoid. It's understandable to divert our gaze from the pain and vulnerability within us, especially in the aftermath of a significant loss. By choosing anger and directing it outward, we unintentionally shield ourselves from recognizing what our heart, mind, and soul truly crave: healing.

It's vital to realize that anger can cloud our judgment and inadvertently distance us from the support of those who genuinely care. We must remember that our truest desire is not to push away our cherished friends, beloved family, or anyone willing to lend a hand during our time of need. Instead, let us open our hearts to compassion, vulnerability, and acceptance, for it is through embracing these qualities that comfort, support, and understanding can be found.

To my readers who have lost a loved one, please do not choose anger or play the blame game. When we lash out at others, that just causes more pain. Choose the path of light and love when dealing with your loss. That is truly the only path to mend your broken heart and find healing and peace. The way to genuine healing is through love.

Another path that we can choose after the loss of a loved one is indifference. Choosing to be indifferent regarding my grief was not an option for me. You see, Indifference to the passing of a loved one is to me—and from what I have seen, and people I have talked to—not healthy either. Suppressing one's emotions can be mentally and spiritually suffocating. My knowledge of the indifferent path of dealing—or NOT dealing—with one's grief is not due to my own personal experience. In fact, my knowledge and understanding of choosing indifference are through the people that I have talked with and have observed. From the people that I have talked to and from what I have observed, suppressing emotions, and choosing to be indifferent about the death of a loved one, is not healthy as well.

There is no healing in denial.

To me, the suppressing of one's emotions is like "kinking off" a garden hose to keep the water from flowing freely. When you kink the hose to stop the water, what happens to the hose and the water? Well . . . in my experience as a master hose sprayer and water balloon champion, what happens is the hose starts to expand, and it bulges with the constricted water. If you have done this before, you will remember what happens to the water. The water tries to escape however it can. It will spit out or squirt out bits or very small streams of water, looking to be set free.

As the hose bulges, it gets more difficult to hold on to and control the water. You see, when the water spicket is turned on, the water starts to flow. That is its natural course and function. When you stop that natural flow, then that is not its proper course. What happens to the hose if you kink it and continue to do this? It can become damaged. Then what happens when you finally release the kinked hose from its confinement? Wow, look out, and don't have your face right in front of it. You will get a rush of water in your face and nose. The hose sprays aggressively and then calms down to—a steady stream, its natural flow. Moreover, the sudden explosion of someone's emotions can have the same effect on others who happen to be in their vicinity, sometimes even manifesting as a violent emotional eruption. Subsequently, as they regain their composure, they find themselves grappling with an entirely different array of challenges, including feelings of guilt and estrangement. These issues might have been avoided if they had simply allowed their emotions to flow naturally.

Using the illustration of kinking a water hose and how detrimental that is to it, we can see how the suppression of the natural flow of emotions can be detrimental to those who mourn. It's important to acknowledge that the more we suppress or disregard our emotions, the harder it becomes to sustain this approach. Take a moment to reflect on individuals you may know who have embarked on this path.

Though they may appear to be handling their grief, they in truth may not be. When someone chooses to suppress or ignore their emotions, it can create an impression of coldness, distance, and of course, indifference. It is difficult to provide comfort or assist someone if they are not willing to acknowledge that they are suffering or that they are in pain. It is my belief, that when someone closes themselves off and refuses to acknowledge what they are feeling after the loss of a loved one, then the healing that they need and so desperately long for, will continue to evade them. Please don't deprive yourself of finding the precious healing that you need by choosing this path.

It's important to recognize that dismissing or denying our feelings and emotions following the loss of a loved one, obstructs the natural ebb and flow of our emotional well-being. Within the pages of this book, I've often emphasized the significance of our emotions as messengers, continuously communicating wisdom to us.

They carry profound significance, and it is essential to honor and listen to what they are telling us. The overwhelming and paralyzing nature of pain after the loss of a loved one makes it tempting to evade and suppress our feelings. It may even seem like a viable option amid our sorrow. However, I believe that such avoidance acts as a mere Band-Aid, attempting to cover the deep well of sorrow within—just like placing a Band-Aid on a twisted water hose. How well could that truly work?

Based on my experience, I have learned it is vital that we allow ourselves to be in touch with our emotions when dealing with our grief. Allowing ourselves to feel and embrace them can be cleansing. It can be a way to release our pain. I feel that the release of our pain through a good cry does assist us. It is cathartic; and many times, it feels good to just cry it out. I know that in my case, this is definitely true. I am sure that many of you can relate to what I'm saying. And I hope that you choose to be in touch with your emotions and let them guide you.

After we lose a loved one, if we let ourselves, we will experience a myriad of emotions, both positive and negative. Some of the negative emotions and feelings that I felt were anger, frustration, irritation, and guilt.

But it is what we do with those negative emotions that is important. I chose to turn my negative feelings into a positive way of dealing with my loss. For example, I took the guilt that I had felt for not doing more, and I let it go. My feeling of guilt was not serving me or anyone else. It was holding me down. I decided to be positive and forgive myself instead, and with the Lord's grace, I turned the guilt that I was feeling into forgiveness.

Choosing light, or the positive path, is to me the only path that leads to true healing. After I decided that it was not working for me to feel guilty or angry, I chose to deal with my grief in a positive way. With much prayer and personal introspection, I chose the path of love and forgiveness.

Forgiveness is a beautiful result of choosing the path of light, or the positive path. I chose the word *light,* because light is the opposite of dark, and it is a path of forgiveness and healing. These are the results that I associate with light—with the path that I knew the Lord wanted me to take. Choosing to travel the positive road requires humility. To let go of our egos and be humble, to be teachable. Throughout my own journey of finding healing and peace, I found the path of light to be illuminating and transformational. With God's help, I chose to move forward in the only way that worked for me and my family, the path of light and love.

The love that I share with Robin and Cheryl, as well as for my beautiful son Daniel, was and is the foundation and motivation for my journey. Knowing and feeling how much I love them always brought me back to where I needed to be while I worked through my grief. I did doubt at times, and I lost sight of what was important. But with their love and support, I would get right back on track.

My faith and my family are what is most important to me and always will be. Family is my support system—my family here, with me in my mortal existence, as well as my family who have returned to their heavenly home. My love for my family is eternal, and I am blessed with the knowledge that I will once again be reunited with my deceased loved ones. My desire to be with them again as an eternal family continually drives me through my journey. What an incredible blessing this knowledge is. I'm sure that many of you who are reading this book, do desire and look forward to being reunited once again with your deceased loved ones as an eternal family.

Love, forgiveness, compassion, and humility were and are all a part of my journey to create healing and loving peace. This ultimately led me to the final part of the light path, peace. I am at peace with where I am in my grief. Reflecting upon the past twenty-eight years, I never imagined I could attain such inner calm after suffering through such incredible loss.

I will always grieve for and miss them. The grieving process never ends. It just gets less painful. Each day, their absence is felt, and I cherish their memories dearly. Yet, amid this grieving process, my heart has found peace. My love for them knows no bounds, transcending time for eternity, and I am blessed that we will be reunited once more. This understanding brings me comfort and calms my soul.

It is my prayer that you will be able to find the healing and peace that you need and desire, as you navigate your own journey of working through your grief.

Love knows not its own depth until
the hour of separation.
—*Kahlil Gibran*

CHAPTER 6

Robin

Sharing My Stories and Experiences with Others

*Sometimes, reaching out and taking
someone's hand is the beginning of a journey.
At other times, it is allowing another to take yours.*
—*Vera Nazarian*

As I wrote earlier in this book, I got to the point where I was choosing to be cautious about the decisions I would make because I had to think about more than just me; I also had to consider how my decisions would affect the boys, especially when I thought about remarrying. I was a young widower, and I did want to marry again. This was a decision that I pondered over greatly; it was an important decision that required a lot of prayer. This was too important of a decision to be made lightly or impulsively. I turned to the Lord for guidance, and my prayers were answered. The Lord blessed me greatly when He brought my second wife, Robin, into my life. She's indeed a gift from above. Robin became a perfect fit for me and our family. God's infinite grace smiled upon me once again.

Robin and I dated for eight months before I was able to place the wedding band on her finger and say, "Yes, I definitely do." The day that I took Robin as my wife was one of the happiest days of my life. I have never met anyone with whom I had more in common than her. Robin is such an incredible blessing to me and my family. From the moment that I first saw her at a singles activity, I knew that I must meet her. We met at a singles dance a week later, and well, we began our journey together. Robin and I built such a strong relationship and marriage throughout the years. Our love and devotion for each other is so incredibly strong. Unfortunately, due to the issues that she had with her health; our earthly life together was cut short.

Robin passed away on January 10, 2019, after suffering from a long-term battle with diabetes and three years after being diagnosed with end-stage renal disease, or kidney failure. Her femoral catheter somehow became dislodged while she was getting ready to go to dialysis. Robin was home by herself. I was working and visiting customers during this time. My mom and dad had planned to pick her up to take her to dialysis like every other Tuesday.

While I was driving to visit another one of my customers, I suddenly felt a need to get home. There was something wrong with Robin. She didn't answer either her cell phone or our home phone, and she failed to respond to my text messages. I was concerned that she might have been in insulin shock.

I sped home to see an ambulance and paramedics in front of my house. My dad, who was there with my mom, knocked on the door, and when there was no answer, he went into our house through the garage. He yelled for Robin and told her they were there to take her to dialysis. No answer. My dad then went upstairs to check on her and found her lying unconscious in a pool of blood in our bathroom. My dad called 911, and then he sat with Robin to comfort her, until the paramedics arrived.

Upon my arrival home, I hurried upstairs to discover my dad in the company of paramedics who were tending to Robin. My beautiful wife lay there motionless in her own blood. She had a faint pulse and was unresponsive. All I could do was watch and pray. They put her into the ambulance and rushed her to the hospital in Lehi, Utah.

Less than an hour later, after several attempts to revive her, the doctor came to tell me that they couldn't stabilize her and that she kept flatlining. He asked if I wanted to have them keep bringing her back. Her blood pressure was dangerously low. I said a prayer for guidance and strength. My heart told me that Robin had suffered enough, that it was time for me to let her go. My tearful heartfelt prayer confirmed what my heart was telling me. Then I told the doctor, *no*, and to just please let her rest, her battle with her failing health was finally over. Robin returned to her heavenly home that day. It was a surreal experience as I watched this beautiful, wonderful woman, my wife, slipping away during her last moments on this earth.

All I could do was caress her face, embrace her, and give her a goodbye kiss. I envisioned her embracing her Lord, and her reunion with her dad, my son Daniel, and other family members who had passed on before her. I was comforted by the knowledge that Robin was no longer in pain. No more finger pricks to test her blood sugar. No more dialysis, and no more trips to the hospital for Robin. She was, indeed, perfect.

Even though the pain of our separation was huge, I was glad that she no longer had to suffer through her health issues. Robin described to me that living day to day with her diabetes felt like she had the flu every day. Imagine that. Along with living with kidney failure, Robin endured so very much. She is my greatest example of enduring to the end, because that is exactly what she did. Her strength and bravery are an example to me, along with the integrity and grace that she embodied as she lived through the many health issues that eventually took her life. I love her so very completely, and I miss her incredibly.

Losing Robin and living with our separation was excruciatingly painful, especially after losing my son Daniel twenty-three months earlier. Her death was not a complete surprise to us, especially because she was in such a weak state; after battling illness for the majority of the previous year. Her struggle with her health in 2018 really zapped her strength and vitality.

We both knew that I would most likely outlive her, but when that became a reality, the pain was so intense and gut-wrenching. My incredible wife of over twenty years was gone. My intense and pure love for Robin got me through the first days after her passing.

Similar to the time when my first wife, Cheryl, and my son, Daniel, passed away, my mind became awash with a torrent of responsibilities and obligations that demanded my attention and care. However, the acute anguish of losing yet another cherished companion returned with a fierce intensity.

As I persisted in my difficult journey of navigating through the aftermath of Robin's death, pain gripped my heart, inflicting a sorrow that was beyond measure. I found myself painfully adding yet another agonizing chapter to the growing story of my grief.

I remember—and this was somewhat humorous at the time—that when my dad and I went to pick out Robin's headstone, I received a "return customer" discount on Robin's headstone. Wow, that was humbling and painful and, like I said, a bit humorous. We had to find the humor in that because it was just surreal. Sitting there, it felt, well, it felt just bizarre. Imagine how that would feel. Imagine the incredible irony of that moment.

After sitting in my car, getting ready to leave the cemetery after my wife Robin's funeral, I thought to myself, Not again. Our marriage is eternal. Our love endures.

For over twenty years Robin and I had done everything together outside of work and my volunteer service. There was no one with whom I would rather be with or do anything with than Robin. We have built such an incredibly loving relationship and a wonderful marriage. Robin's my best friend as well as my wife. That is more than just a cliché to me. But that seems like such an understatement, so inadequate a description. We have such a deep understanding of each other's souls, and have always possessed a deeper understanding of each other than anyone else on this planet. Robin is my soulmate in all the essence and intensity of what that describes.

When Robin passed away and returned to her heavenly home, I was devastated. Love this pure and intense is incredible, and it lasts forever. Now I had to adjust from having her here physically with me to expressing my affection for her in different ways—in a more eternal and spiritual way, if you will.

Sharing with others verbally, as well as in writing, are ways that I have chosen to honor my deceased loved ones. When I share my stories about them with others, I honor them. I am sharing not only a piece of them with others, but I am also sharing a part of the love that I hold for them. They are always with me in spirit, and here by my side when I need them. The memories and feelings that I share show my love and affection for my loved ones, absolutely.

Every time I experience the loss of a beloved family member, it is profoundly personal and heart-wrenching. The process of healing and finding a way to carry on has proven to be challenging. I take solace in knowing that their departure has freed them from the burden of physical pain. When we lose a loved one, we must find the resilience to navigate our own unique path forward through our grief. Opening up and sharing my story with others is one way that I have found to be useful and healing.

As I mentioned earlier, this act of sharing has been incredibly cathartic for me and has been so beneficial for the healing of my heart. As I contemplate my journey, it becomes clear to me that many of my actions were, indeed, a way of sharing the stories of my loved ones' passing. Even though at the time it didn't feel very cathartic, it felt more like the relaying of information. But the condolences and support that I received were indeed comforting and provided me with some healing as well.

This began with reaching out to my family and friends, informing them about the events that had transpired and how my loved ones departed from this world.

One of the first things I had to take care of was organizing their funerals, which included their obituaries and my talks at their funeral services, along with asking others to speak as well. Funerals are for us, the living, to remember and honor those who have gone on before us. When my son Daniel passed away, I wanted to, and I had to, speak at his funeral, as I put it in my talk, "To Mark the Moment," my honorable son returned to his Heavenly Father. To mark the moment, and to tell the world how I loved and honored my son Daniel and to honor his life. He is my son, and I felt it important to share how much I loved him. Daniel, with the pureness of his heart, touched many people's lives.

Funerals can be a last goodbye for some and a continuation of love and affection in a different way for others. Remember yourself at your loved one's funeral. When you reminisce about that day, feel it; don't think it. Get in touch with what you felt and what you now feel. Take time to write down your feelings and the memories that you experienced on the day when you said your last goodbye to your loved one before they were laid to rest. Listen to your heart and allow yourself to feel it.

As you look back, what do you now feel? How has your grief changed? You can write your feelings and memories down in a "grief journal" as I have chosen to do. These feelings and memories are something that you can share with others however you wish. There are times that I like to go back and read through the thoughts and feelings that I have written down in my own grief journal, it does assist, and it is very healing. Whenever I feel inspired, I still write about what my heart is feeling about my deceased loved ones in my journal. Let your heart be your guide.

During each of those moments, when I uttered my last earthly farewell and said my goodbyes to Cheryl, Daniel, and Robin, I embraced a transformed connection with them. How we choose to move forward from that moment is deeply personal to each of us, and how we determine to move forward resides within our own hearts, with our departed loved ones, and with God. Grief is a journey, unique to each of us. We all grieve in our own distinct ways, experiencing a myriad of emotions and thoughts as we navigate through the process of healing.

We can learn from each other and how we are dealing with our grief after our loss. That is the purpose of my writing this book. So that you may learn from my experiences and the lessons that I have learned while working through my grief. Losing your loved one is the most painful thing anyone can go through in this lifetime. I have experienced a plethora of emotions and have had many incredible and profound experiences throughout my journey of finding healing and peace. It is not arrogant for me to say that I gained a lot of wisdom while working through my grief. With assistance from God and my loved ones, I have. I'm hoping that you can take from my journey anything that can help you as you take your own journey, and work through your own grief after losing someone dear to you.

The condolences and well wishes that I received helped me greatly, especially when we would reminisce about Robin, Cheryl, or Daniel, it was comforting. The love and affection that I felt while sharing with others did a lot to heal me. Since Daniel passed away, my youngest son, Samuel, and I have had a lot of talks about Daniel. We would talk about our memories of him and the Rush concerts that the three of us attended together. That is one of my fondest memories—being able to attend a concert of my favorite rock band, Rush, with my sons. It was incredible fun, especially being able to share these moments with them. Samuel and I would talk about how Daniel died and what led up to it, how we both felt, and how we loved him. Our many shared memories of Daniel provide us with a strong bond.

Whether it was sharing in a support group or with family and friends, I want to emphasize again to you how much it helps and how healing it is to share. To put it plainly, sharing our stories and feelings with others, lightens and heals the heart. The support and affection you receive when expressing your emotions about your departed loved one can offer you comfort and contribute to the healing of your heart.

My parents have a special relationship with Daniel. He had gotten really close to them before he passed. My dad would assist Daniel every month with his finances. Whenever they called Daniel on the phone and asked for his assistance with some chores or anything, Daniel readily went to help them. I know that he really loves his Nanny and Pappa.

Daniel's death hit my parents very hard. We like to reminisce about him and how he has such a kind heart. "He has no malice to anyone," my dad will say. Sharing with each other gives us support, comfort, and strength. It is very healing.

Initially, I was hesitant to participate in support meetings following the loss of my wife Cheryl. I reluctantly attended a few but quickly gave up on the idea. However, after Daniel's passing, I found myself drawn back to those meetings. I felt they provided some assistance, but the ones I attended were held in a medical or mental health facility. They had a more clinical atmosphere and adopted a standardized approach to addressing grief as if it could be universally treated. While I acknowledge that pain can be a shared experience, I found these meetings too detached and impersonal. We shared our stories and then dissected them according to the prescribed steps of grief. Unfortunately, this method didn't resonate with me. I desired something more profound—an alternative approach that would help me navigate through my grief.

Experiencing pain, guilt, sadness, or any range of emotions is an inherent part of the human condition, as they are often emphasized in those support meetings. While I understand they were there to provide me with support and comfort, they lacked the personal touch I was seeking. It felt like a generic approach rather than one tailored to the uniqueness of my own grief. I'm certain that many of you who have attended similar support meetings may relate to this sentiment. Once again, from my perspective, grief is an intensely personal journey that cannot be effectively generalized if we desire something beyond mere consolation. In my case, I thought I was selfish and maybe a bit weird for wanting more—for wanting more than just a clinical approach to grief. Support meetings are not bad or ineffective, they just didn't work for me.

I yearned for something greater. I longed for healing, forgiveness, and the ability to grieve in my own way. I sought a path that resonated with my needs, as I forged ahead, seeking healing, forgiveness, and a renewed sense of clarity.

This came to me by looking deeper into myself and wanting to do more than just be comforted. From my perspective and based on my own experiences, I have come to understand that a profound sense of comfort emerges hand in hand with healing and forgiveness, which brings to us clarity, all under the wonderful embrace of love.

After Robin's death, sharing my experiences and feelings on social media took off more intensely. I shared about my loved ones, usually on their birthdays or anniversaries of their passing as well as holidays. When Robin first passed away, I usually shared several times a week, because each time I shared my feelings about her, it assisted in my healing, and it still does. Whenever my heart called for it, I opened up about my thoughts and emotions regarding my departed loved ones.

The first week after Robin passed away, I received a lot of wonderful, kind responses to my social media posts during that week. I even printed them out and displayed them next to the sign-in book at her viewing and funeral service. I was touched and in awe of the many people who reached out to me and my family during this incredibly difficult time. I even got condolences from people who I didn't know, on social media. I sometimes go back and read them. They still give me comfort and a warm feeling. I hope that you would consider doing the same with the condolences and well wishes that were written to you about your deceased loved one. Reading back through the condolences that you received can be comforting and can assist you in your healing. From my experience, they definitely do.

Whenever I opened up on social media, whether it was about my son Daniel or my cherished wives Cheryl and Robin, something remarkable happened. Friends and acquaintances of Daniel, Cheryl, and Robin came forward, to share their personal stories and memories that they had of them. It warms my heart to read how much Daniel's friends loved him and wanted to honor him. Daniel has so many good friends who care for him a lot.

Social media is, as I have experienced, a good platform to share about your deceased loved ones, sharing your thoughts, feelings, and memories. It creates an opportunity for others within the online community to respond with an outpouring of love and support. I'm sure many of you can relate to what I'm saying, if you have shared your feelings and memories on social media about a loved one whom you have lost. The warm and affectionate responses that you receive are a humbling and genuinely beautiful experience. As a part of my journey to healing, this helped me in mending my broken heart.

As I've previously written, I have found that expressing myself and sharing with others out there in this social media world, if you will, is healing and cathartic. I know that when I write down what I am feeling and what I want to say about my deceased loved ones, it really assists me a ton and is very healing for me.

There is a quote about sharing with others from one of my favorite BBC shows, *Monarch of the Glen*[5] The quote was from the show's character Archie McDonald when he was asked to share with others in a healing session, his reply was: "Ah right, colonic irrigation for the soul." To me, sharing is good for the soul, and it can cleanse sorrow from our hearts. Remembering our loved ones and releasing our emotions and feelings for them is something that I have experienced while sharing. I have also felt my loved ones' presence while I am sharing with others. This is warm and comforting.

As I have previously written, when we share, it's not just the positive memories that surface. We also recount instances of challenges and hardships as we open up to those around us. While it may seem challenging, this type of sharing is also beneficial, for not all memories can be entirely positive. The truth, in all its facets, holds importance in our process of navigating grief. They help us appreciate the shared struggles we endured and how we worked to overcome them together. This truly can become a positive and freeing experience throughout our journey.

Sharing our stories, feelings, experiences, and the lessons that we learned, in any way or on any platform, can be cathartic. When you share with others throughout your own journey, it is my firm belief that this will help you find the healing that you desire and need—the healing and clarity that can eventually bring you peace of mind and spirit after the loss of your loved one.

When you are sharing with others, about your feelings and the love that you have in your heart for your deceased loved one. Get in touch with those feelings and the joy that you experience while sharing. The warmth that fills you, the genuine feeling of love that is filling your soul. Embrace this warmth and the joy that you are feeling. It is beautiful, it is healing, and it lightens your heart.

When you share your thoughts and feelings,
you connect with others, and that's the first
step in becoming part of a community.
—Brian Eno

CHAPTER 7

Find a Place of Refuge

Being Alone with Your Thoughts and Feelings

Inner stillness is the key to outer strength.
—*Jared Brock*

Throughout my journey, I found it necessary to take time for myself. A time of self-reflection and to calm my mind and spirit—to calm my soul, if you will. Through the hustle and bustle of life's daily responsibilities, along with dealing with my grief, it was, and still is, important for me to find a place where I can be alone and center myself—to be still. This is of vital importance to me; it is a time when I can "take stock" of where I am in my grief.

With all the business and day-to-day responsibilities of life that I had, it was easy for me to lose sight of where I was, when dealing with my grief. Taking time for self-care allowed me to recharge, refocus, and reaffirm my course along my journey to find healing and eventually peace. I went to a place of refuge, or my "sanctuary", to be still and to take the time I needed for myself. A place where I could be alone with my thoughts and my feelings. Where I could be alone with my Heavenly Father and my deceased loved ones, receiving inspiration, strength, and comfort from them.

It is a good place to be still.
—*Reverend Mitchell,* Monarch of the Glenn *TV series*

I remember many times when I was struggling or just kind of stuck in dealing with my grief. I would go to the cemetery where my loved ones are interned, to sit and be still. For me it is a sacred place—hallowed ground. Being next to their final resting places is sacred to me and is one of my places of refuge. It really is a humbling experience, and I feel very close to them when I am there.

I know that it is just their mortal remains that are there, but their graves are places of prayer. Prayer, feelings, and emotions are a part of this sacred space. A prayer was said to dedicate their graves when they were laid to rest. When I am there on this hallowed ground, I often offer silent prayers of gratitude. For I am very grateful to my Heavenly Father, for bringing these beautiful souls into my life. It is to me a place where I can slow my thoughts while being still.

While I am at my place of refuge, I like to listen to music and meditate or center myself. I often listen to music when I just want to sit quietly and "be still". The type of music I like to listen to, while I am at my place of refuge is Celtic, Native American, soft folk music, and instrumental meditation music. This music calms me.

When I want to be still and center myself, I like to go to scenic areas like the Wasatch Mountains or sit by a lake or stream. Being there in awe of the glorious wonder of God's creation is humbling and gives me a space where I can think and feel. Being alone and still in nature is very serene. Being in this stillness really does give my mind some rest, and I am able to center my thoughts. The lakes are splendid and beautiful. Sitting there by the edge of the lake, listening to the water splash on the rocks or shore, to me is very relaxing. The calming sound takes the edge off my day and helps me relax. It is majestic looking over a lake. Watching the birds and other wildlife is a nice way to spend some introspective, thoughtful time.

The time in nature while refocusing and recharging adds beautifully to my getting in touch with where I am in my grief at that moment, and this helps me to see where I need to focus in order to move forward.

There were times when I just couldn't do it, couldn't take it anymore, and when grief dominated my life. Times when I was frustrated, bewildered, and overwhelmed because I was dealing with all the crazy, frustrating aspects of life, all while endeavoring to make progress. At those times, I found time to go to my place of refuge and be calm. It felt so good to tune out the world for a brief time and be still. Oh, wow, to be able to charge my batteries, refocus myself, and gain strength. I'm sure that many of you can relate to what I'm saying here. It's difficult to find time for yourself. In my personal experience, it's essential to find moments for solitude and self-reflection, focus on yourself, charge your batteries, and regroup. This benefits not only us but our family as well.

Setting aside moments for solitude has a profoundly calming effect on my soul. I look inward and engage in self-reflection, confronting my grief and seeking solace. The experience is not only humbling but also deeply enlightening, creating a sense of spiritual peace that resonates within me. This dedicated time for myself leaves an enduring, calming imprint on my inner being. I also take spiritual reading material like the scriptures with me as well. Reading the words of the Lord's prophets, or other inspired writings, is very helpful to me during my time of introspection. When I was finished and ready to go, I felt lighter, and I was ready to continue my journey of working through my grief. This was a much-needed time for me to take for myself to find healing and peace. This time of self-reflection focuses my mind and brings me clarity. Taking this much-needed time for ourselves also lightens our hearts and edifies our spirits. It definitely assists us with taking on life.

We can all choose where our place of refuge is. The cemetery and nature are places that work for me. Choose where you want as your refuge, a place where you can be still. This looks different for everyone. Whatever place you choose, make it yours. It is a place where you can be calm and become centered.

This is one of the aspects that I used throughout my journey. I still go to my places of refuge where I can be still when I feel the need. If you feel that this works for you, then I would invite you to find that place where you can go and be still, your place of refuge, your sanctuary. Where you can be quiet, where you can feel. The place where you can go to recharge and continue your journey toward healing and peace. It doesn't matter where you go or where you choose for your sanctuary. What matters the most is that you are taking time for yourself. Time to center yourself, to "take stock" of where you are in dealing with your grief.

Wherever you choose as your refuge, this is your space to be still and calm. These reflective moments that you spend in your sanctuary will allow you to not lose focus or become lost during your journey. I feel that this will assist you with recharging your batteries—like when your TV remote control is low on juice because the batteries are low. When you use your remote, it responds slower and is erratic. It can be very frustrating when it is not working properly because the batteries are drained. This is akin to your energy waning as you navigate through the challenges of grief and daily life—it gets busy and hectic. Life happens. It is important to take time for yourself, both mentally and spiritually.

It is a good self-awareness tool. Normally our minds are always working, and thinking about what we need to do that day, whether it be work, school, our family and our kids' school or sports activities, or our civic or spiritual responsibilities. Our day is so chock full of everything we need to accomplish, and it can be overwhelming. I am sure that you can appreciate what I am saying. I had my usual daily responsibilities and activities while I was "trying" to deal with my grief. Remember what Master Yoda said to Luke in *Star Wars: The Empire Strikes Back*: "Do or do not. There is no try."

I was "trying" and not succeeding. I was attempting to work through my grief while my mind was everywhere else. It is possible to deal with your grief and go through your normal life, but we all need to find time for ourselves to be alone and take a breath. We can also look at it as regrouping. I needed to find time for myself during the chaos of life. Finding time for myself to be still, was a good way for me to regain focus. When I couldn't find time to go to my place of refuge, I would sometimes just shut the door to my bedroom, put on music, and take time for myself there. Again, it doesn't matter where you choose to go to be still. It just matters that you do take the time for yourself.

Many times, while I was at my place of refuge, I would write in my grief journal or record my thoughts and feelings.

Many things I wrote or recorded became a part of this book. When my mind is calm, I can feel my deceased loved ones close by. This allows me to have a continual personal connection with them. Once more, slow down and be still while you are navigating your own journey toward healing. If this resonates with you, get in touch with it and witness the immense benefits it can bring to you.

As I wrote earlier, I loved to listen to music during my journey. Music is a great reminder of our deceased loved ones. Some songs remind me of them; like a song played at their viewing or funeral service.

Music can bring back thoughts and memories. This can easily happen when we hear that certain song that reminds us of them. I am sure that you have experienced being somewhere when a song plays that reminds you of your deceased loved one—songs that remind you of the love and the moments you shared together. While the song is playing, the memories flood back and wash all over you.

There is one song that I used for my son's collage of memories—the collage of pictures of my son for his viewing and funeral. I first heard this song after my son died; it still has a profound effect on me. This song still brings up powerful emotions for me. The song that I am referencing is "A Parent's Lullaby" by Camilyn Morrison.

It is a beautiful song, especially for parents who have lost a child. If you want and need a good cry, this song will help you do that. I miss my son very much. It reminds me of his pure heart and that he is always with me, watching over me.

The healing that we can find begins with the knowledge that we will be with our deceased loved ones again. And that they are always here to watch over us.

Music is an incredible medium that taps into our emotions and our feelings. Usually, when we least expect it, a song will play that reminds us of our love for them. Music is a powerful reminder. Wow, yes, a very powerful reminder indeed. Yep, there are times when I'm listening to music, and that song comes on. And of course, I must sing along, badly, much to the chagrin of my kids or whoever is in the car with me. Believe me, for the others in my car it is not a pleasant experience, but that song brings back memories to me that I cherish.

Music hath power to bring out my terrible singing voice.

Some Rush songs remind me of the time when my sons and I attended their concerts together. These songs bring back the cherished memory of being able to share these wonderful experiences with my boys.

The tools I have discussed in this chapter have proven invaluable in my personal journey. Finding a place of refuge where you can be still and reflect, or just be in the moment of still calmness, a place of your own—a place to be alone and take time for yourself. Cultivating a state of calmness provides an opportunity to regain focus and gain clarity on your path of healing after the loss of your loved one. Take time to clear the mind, to feel, and to get in touch with your spirit. Listen to your heart, experience the calmness of the moment, and center yourself, aligning your mind and heart together.

Music is relaxing and it can help you align yourself; it can be uplifting for you while you're in your place of sanctuary. I like to think of it as music that speaks to your spirit. which continues to be a great source of comfort for me.

I also wrote about songs that remind us of the times we shared with our deceased loved ones—the songs that bring the memories flooding back. As I stated earlier, grief doesn't end—it doesn't go away. It gets less acute and less painful. We can go from dealing with and working through our grief to living with it. It will always be with us. For our loved ones are a part of us, always.

I invite you to use anything that I have shared with you in this chapter if you feel that it will assist you. Because I have found that calming our minds and spirits is valuable to us. Definitely do what works for you. Finding healing and peace is not easy. Many times, while dealing with grief and living life, things seem to spiral out of control, and you feel overwhelmed. It is in these moments that taking time for yourself can be truly beneficial. This allows you to regenerate yourself and to continue your journey to find healing and peace.

Music washes away from the soul
the dust of everyday life.
—Berthold Auerbach

CHAPTER 8

Letting Go of Guilt

The Spiritual Focus of My Healing, Part 1

Guilt is always hungry, don't let it consume you.
— *Terri Guillemets*

As I navigated my path toward healing, the spiritual aspect of my journey has consistently played a significant role. Central to this journey is my unwavering faith and belief system. At the core of my faith lies the profound understanding that our existence transcends the physical realm and continues on, even after death. Through our Savior's resurrection from the dead, we know that this gift is given to us through his infinite love and mercy. This knowledge, which is a part of my faith, is a great comfort to me and those of us "left behind." Knowing that I will be with my loved ones forever and envisioning our glorious reunion has been, and is, a vital part of my journey.

I can't imagine not knowing this—not knowing that I will see my loved ones again. Thinking that there was nothing after we die . . . Not having this knowledge would be extremely empty and lonely. To me, this is a cold and frightful thought.

Not being able to see my loved ones again would be unsettling, and it would suck big time if death were the end—if that were all. Never being able to be with them again is unimaginable.

It is wonderful to have the knowledge that we will live on after we die, and that families are forever. For we do live on; we can be with our loved ones again. This knowledge is a blessing. And I thank God every day for that knowledge. After I leave this mortal existence and return to my heavenly home, I will be able to walk up to them, look them in the eyes, and with a big smile, embrace them once again. This is comforting to me and fills me with eternal gratitude and *joy*.

I am so grateful for the knowledge that we have of the resurrection and being able to be with our loved ones again. I'm very grateful for my faith and how it has sustained me throughout my life, especially after losing my beautiful son and my two wonderful wives. Just saying that I am grateful is a complete understatement. There really are no words in the English language that can properly describe how grateful I am, that I will be reunited with them once again. This is, indeed, humbling, and beautiful. I'm sure that many of you can relate to what I am saying.

I am also very grateful for the life that we had together on this earth—a lot of happy and wondrous times. There is nothing that I enjoy more than spending time with my family—going on vacations, and road trips, playing video games, playing in the yard with our children, spending time watching TV, going to the movies and rock concerts with my sons, and many other fun activities we enjoy. I particularly have fond memories of our vacation to Disneyland and SeaWorld when our children were young, as well as our road trips to St. George, Utah, then on to Area 51 and the Lil' Alien Inn in Nevada, along with the many other vacations that we took as a family.

The most wonderful and powerful experience that any couple can share is the birth of their child. In my opinion, it is the closest we can come to heaven as mortals. I am eternally grateful for my family and what they mean to me, for the times we spent together and the life that we shared here on earth.

I'm not going to blow smoke up your skirt here and stay with the illusion that all the years of our lives together were always joyous and happy. They were not always happy and sunshine, lollipops, unicorns, rainbows, and Sasquatches. There were also times of frustration and sadness—less joyful times. We as human beings all have our trials and tough times. There are times when everything is not so rosy under the sun, when we drive our spouses nuts, and vice versa. Times when our children test our patience, times when we are angry and sad. Yes, our family had all of those, and I'm sure yours has as well. We are all individuals with our own quirks and idiosyncrasies. We are not perfect, nor should we pretend to be. This is all part of raising a family and the human experience.

But being able to work through the tough times, the sad times, as a couple and a family, provides us with the lessons learned as a spouse and as parents. After losing Daniel, I have often thought about the invaluable lessons that I learned throughout his life before he returned to his heavenly home. I am glad for the times when it took courage, strength, and forgiveness to work through the rough patches that we had.

It was very important for me to extend forgiveness to myself and others as I traveled throughout my journey of working through my grief. Forgiveness is something that the Savior taught—that we were to forgive others whom we think have wronged us.

> *For if ye forgive men their trespasses, your*
> *heavenly Father will also forgive you.*
> —Mathew 6:14

Following the loss of my loved ones, I experienced a certain degree of *guilt* after their passing. After the death of a loved one, we are not always rational. I'm sure those of you who have lost someone can understand and appreciate this. Guilt is a typical emotion that people have after the loss of a loved one. The feeling of guilt didn't serve me at all. To me, based on my experience, guilt is not an emotion that supports moving forward to find healing and peace.

It was different with each of my loved ones who passed away. When my first wife, Cheryl, and my son Daniel passed away, I felt guilty about what I could have possibly done to prevent it. Could I have done more for them? What did I do that may have contributed to their mindset when they took their own lives? Was I supportive enough? I know I'm not alone in having these kinds of feelings and thoughts after losing someone. But these feelings were in my mind, and they were not helping me at all.

After Cheryl passed away, I felt guilty about not supporting her enough. I knew that her emotional and psychological state was becoming worse and more fragile. I often asked myself, "Could I have done more?" She had dealt with so much in her young life. I felt guilty about what I perceived as abandoning her after our divorce. Guilt clouded my emotions and feelings.

So, with prayer and much introspection, I let go of it—I let go of the guilt. I did find forgiveness for myself, and for anyone else with whom I felt that I needed to extend my forgiveness. Letting go of guilt and embracing forgiveness truly lightened my heart.

After Daniel passed away, guilt found its way back into my mind and into my consciousness, as it did when his mom passed away. Could I have done more to assist Daniel? Could I have listened to him more? What could I have done to possibly prevent his death? Was I a good father to him? I again decided that guilt was not doing anything except clouding my ability to find forgiveness once again.

I did find forgiveness for myself after my son returned to his heavenly home. I also needed to extend forgiveness to Cheryl and Daniel for taking their own lives. I understood the whys, and I didn't blame them. But a part of me still needed to forgive them so I could truly move forward—to be in complete alignment with them emotionally, mentally, and spiritually. To be one with them.

After my second wife Robin passed, it's understandable that I initially felt guilty and questioned whether I should have been there with her during that difficult time as she lay bleeding out from her dislodged dialysis catheter. At first, I thought that I should have been there with her. But that guilt didn't serve me either. Robin's death, as painful as it was, was not really a surprise to us due to her failing health, her lifelong battle with diabetes, and her struggle with kidney failure. Robin spent a good portion of 2018 in various medical facilities as a result of her various health issues. She ended that year in a weakened physical condition. That year was the last Christmas we celebrated with Robin. Just over two weeks later, she passed away.

I remember many times when I was in prayer and asking my Heavenly Father to bless Robin regarding her declining health because she was suffering and in pain, with incredible daily discomfort. I prayed for our Father in Heaven to assist Robin with her suffering, and to help her with her debilitating and declining health. We were hoping for a miracle in the form of a kidney and pancreas transplant.

She was on the shortlist for a kidney transplant. I remember the day she passed away, as I was leaving to follow the ambulance to the ER. I thought about her being in such pain and how she made such frequent trips to the ER and hospital. Watching Robin slip away physically was so difficult for me and my family. So, with pure love in my heart, I said a prayer to my Heavenly Father as I left for the ER: "Heavenly Father, if you're going to take her soon anyway, and if it be thy will, please just take her now. She has suffered so much." I wanted her to be free of her pain and daily suffering. I wasn't praying for her to die; I was praying for her relief. My heart was in such pain, watching her endure through her failing health. Robin is the strongest woman I have ever known, and such a wonderful example to me, and my family. I love her with every fiber of my soul.

God took her home that day—she was no longer in pain. Her release, and finally being free from her declining health, was truly a miracle. She was finally released from the grip of her debilitating health issues. For this, I am eternally grateful.

I have found through my experiences with loss that if we have feelings of guilt, we need to deal with them and let them go because guilt can eat us up. There really is no path to healing, through harboring feelings of guilt. I'm grateful to say that my feelings of guilt didn't last long. As I previously said, I chose to let them go, for they were not serving me. I know that it is not easy to let go of the guilt. But with faith and God's help, we can,

I addressed my feelings of guilt and discovered forgiveness through various approaches, yet I believe that prayer stands out as the most significant of them all. By humbly approaching my Heavenly Father in prayer, I was able to start dealing with the feelings of guilt that I had. Through prayer, I knew that He did not want me to feel this way and was there for me anytime that I needed him.

Throughout my journey toward healing, faith and prayer were the most vital components to me when dealing with my feelings of guilt. The support and strength that I received from my Heavenly Father were the foundation of my working through my grief. Knowing that *I* was *never alone* when I was in mourning and hurting, and during my toughest moments, and my most difficult days. This is so comforting to me. Prayer is our conduit to God, to ask Him for the support, wisdom, and strength that we need. He is there, and He is just waiting for us to reach out to Him.

Each of us may hold diverse faiths or belief systems, and it's natural for our beliefs to vary. Turning to our own individual faiths and spirituality can provide us with the guidance we seek. When a life is abruptly cut short due to violence or an accident, a multitude of questions arise. It is during these challenging times that faith and prayer play a vital role, offering us inspiration and strength to navigate through the depths of our questions.

I know that when I struggled and had questions, I would seek answers in the Holy Scriptures, as well as inspired talks and writings from God's servants here on earth. The words from the Lord's prophets, as well as other inspired writings, are so beneficial to me and they assisted me greatly during my darkest hours.

My sincere wish and prayer are that you can draw from my experiences and the wisdom I've gathered on my own journey, to aid you in navigating your path toward healing and peace. I encourage you to lean on your faith and reach out to your higher power as you navigate through the journey of your grief.

Letting go of any guilt that you may be holding on to, will unburden your heart, allowing you to find forgiveness and healing.

Guilt is a heavy burden that weighs down the
spirit. Release it and allow yourself to soar.
—*Unknown*

CHAPTER 9

Finding Forgiveness

The Spiritual Focus of My Healing, Part 2

*Forbearing one another, and forgiving one
another, if any man have a quarrel against any:
even as Christ forgave you, so also do ye.*
—Colossians 3:13

*Forgiveness is not forgetting.
It is remembering and letting go.*
—Alexandra Aspinall

As I have written, music has been a very invaluable source of comfort and inspiration to me, as I moved forward through my grief. The song "Show Me the Way" by the rock group Styx really touched me. It is a beautiful song—I frequently listened to it throughout my healing journey.

Finding forgiveness in my heart allowed me to move forward and work through my grief toward healing and peace. Freeing myself from guilt and finding forgiveness was vital to my healing. Not only did I feel that I needed to forgive myself, but I needed to forgive others as well.

I found that I was angry with the mental health doctors who treated Cheryl and Daniel. I played the "blame game," and I blamed them for playing a part in the mental and neurological decline of my wife and son. I realized through prayer and study that blaming others is a way to avoid looking at ourselves and even at our loved ones. That can be a natural reaction but not at all healthy.

Fortunately for me, I didn't play the blame game for long, and when Robin died, I didn't look to place blame anywhere. I guess that may have been because I was more mature by then. I had a better understanding of loss when Robin passed away. I know that I had gained some wisdom by then. At least I'd like to think so. I did learn from my experiences, from the losses of Cheryl and Daniel. I can most assuredly say, that a lot of the wisdom that I have gained came from the inspiration that I received from my Heavenly Father.

As I have written about before in this book, I decided that the anger and blame didn't serve me, so I committed myself to work to forgive. I held the Savior as my example in this: If He can ask the Father to forgive those who nailed him to the cross, then I can assuredly forgive those I was angry with. *I want to say here that I am in no way comparing myself to our Savior, what I am saying is that I wanted to follow his example of forgiveness.*

To free my heart, I needed to forgive.

Forgiveness is a vital part of the road forward to healing and peace. I found that forgiving myself and others after the loss of my loved ones also gave me incredible freedom. I became free of the guilt and anger that held me down. Anger and guilt are like weights or chains that we have chosen to put on ourselves.

Imagine moving through life with an incredible weight of guilt. Like being weighed down and restricted by heavy chains around your shoulders and arms. The mere act of moving through existence becomes an arduous task. The weight of these chains hinders your every motion, limiting your agility and impeding your natural range of movement. This state of restriction becomes a constant source of discomfort, imposing severe limitations on your arms and shoulders. Your limbs feel constrained, numbed by the chains' unyielding grip, effectively reducing your ability to reach and grasp. Even the simple act of reaching out for something or connecting with others becomes a formidable challenge as the shackles bind you, rendering such endeavors immensely difficult, where you are held captive.

Contrast this with the profound discomfort and constraints we experience when burdened by the guilt and anger that we have placed upon ourselves. These emotions restrict our actions and abilities, hindering us from being able to forgive. Consider the acute anguish caused by the loss of a loved one and how, by consciously choosing to carry an overwhelming load of guilt and anger, we prevent ourselves from seeking support from others. Instead of reaching out for support or sharing our emotions honestly, we allow anger to dictate our interactions. We refrain from accepting the embrace and assistance offered by those around us, having metaphorically chained ourselves off from genuine connection and shutting ourselves off from the healing power of human connection. I have felt that myself. Whoa, I can remember how it felt to me. It sucked! I hated it. I had to do something about it. Argh! I had to let it go, cast it off, and forgive. I had to throw off the yolk of guilt to forgive myself and let go of anger so that I could forgive others.

Deciding that this simply doesn't work, that this is not serving us, and that this is holding us back from moving forward through our grief to healing—that is a vitally important step in dealing with our grief. Ah, yeah, to be finally rid of these chains and be free. Wow, can you just get in touch with how it will feel when we throw off this yolk that has kept us captive? FREEDOM! In forgiveness, we can find freedom.

It's not an easy journey, to get to a place
where you forgive people. But it is such a
powerful place because it frees you.
—*Tyler Perry*

As I have stated before, I found assistance in my journey toward healing in the Holy Scriptures. They gave me hope that I possess the strength to triumph over any adversity. When confronted with the overwhelming weight of grief, the path to healing initially appeared daunting and almost insurmountable. Doubts crept in, whispering to me that overcoming this sorrow was an impossible feat, that it was just too difficult. But thankfully I found inspiration within the Holy Scriptures.

There are many stories of faith and forgiveness that helped me—the story that has inspired and uplifted me the most, of course, is the story and life of our Savior, Jesus Christ. The stories of him healing the sick and the accounts of his many miracles uplifted and inspired me, as I traveled my journey. I also could be healed. My broken heart could be mended. God could and would, heal me, after my loss, all I had to do was ask. My healing didn't come quickly, but with my Heavenly Father's assistance, it did.

The life of the Savior is such an example to me. What he went through, his atonement, and that he gave himself as a sacrifice for us all. His resurrection gave us all the blessing of being able to live on after we die—to be resurrected and reunited with our loved ones once again. What an incredible comfort that is to me. It is a beacon for me to navigate through my journey, knowing that my loved ones are there for me and supporting me, as I move forward on my path of working through my grief, to forgiveness and healing. Our deceased loved ones can give us much strength on our path to finding peace.

With these wonderful resources, I was strengthened, inspired, and edified. They spoke not only to my mind but to my heart. Many of the writings I read were from authors who are members of my own faith, as well as from authors outside my faith. These authors take a faith-based approach to their message and, indeed, helped me throughout my journey.

I hope that you find inspiration in the Holy Scriptures or in inspirational writings, as I have. Yet ultimately, it depends on us, and our readiness to embrace and navigate through our sorrow. There are no shortcuts—no easy fixes—if you want to truly face your grief and work through it toward healing. Faith and prayer are a compass and a light that can illuminate your journey, especially when you need to find your way through the darkness. It is through God's guidance and His infinite mercy that we can find forgiveness and lighten our hearts.

The bottom line of my book is that *I never lost my faith.* Throughout the tragedies from the deaths of my two beloved wives and my wonderful son, I never lost or doubted my faith. I kept my faith and my love for my Heavenly Father. I never doubted Him. That is something I am incredibly grateful for.

Forgiveness leads to the freeing of one's heart.
—Lloyd C. Davis

CHAPTER 10

Family and Friends

Support, Comfort, and Strength

Family is not an important thing. It's everything.
—Michael J. Fox

Family

This chapter is about how much my family and friends helped me to find healing and peace, while experiencing the incredible tragedy of losing my two wives and my son. Throughout my journey, my family was vital to me, as they still are today. Like any other aspect of my journey, my family was an integral part of my working through my grief to find healing and peace. This chapter is dedicated to family and friends and the part they play in our lives, especially the assistance that they give us during our darkest days. When our grief and pain overwhelm us, family and friends are indispensable and they add color and meaning to our lives, providing us with love, support, and a sense of belonging. They are the ones who celebrate our joys, stand by us during challenging times, and help us grow into the best versions of ourselves. Their presence creates a strong support system that uplifts us, reminding us that *we are never alone* on this journey we call life.

While you work through your grief to find healing and peace, your family and friends can travel that journey with you. Please reach out to them for strength and comfort. They are your support system. They can lighten your burden and assist you along your journey to find healing and, ultimately, find peace in your grief.

To me, family is everything. As both an earthly and eternal unit, family is, to me, most important; aside from God and from our Savior, family is where I get my greatest strength and support.

When my son Daniel passed away, Robin, was indispensable to me; assisting me with taking care of everything that I needed to do for the funeral arrangements, such as picking out the casket and the headstone, as well as helping me with the obituary and the program for Daniel's memorial service. She was invaluable to me in dealing with all the logistics of what had to be taken care of when Daniel passed away. Robin was an incredible strength, support, and comfort to me as I mourned my son.

Other things may change us, but we
start and end with the family.
—Anthony Brandt

Derrick, Samuel, & Elizabeth

During my journey to find healing, my three children still with me on this earth were incredibly helpful to me, and I thank God for them every day.

Derrick, who, as I wrote earlier, is our oldest and has Down syndrome. He has such an innocence about him. The unconditional love that he shows to all of us is comforting and inspiring. He loves his mom, Cheryl, his siblings, and his second mom, Robin, very much. The pure love that he had for his moms and his brother after they passed away was all so evident in the emotions that he exhibited. Derrick was very close to Cheryl before she passed, and he still is. I gave him a framed picture of Cheryl on Christmas; he loves that picture of her so much. He will place the picture of her in different parts of his grandparents' home. He mostly likes to have it in his bedroom. It is my feeling that the picture of his mom gives Derrick a lot of comfort, and he will often say his mom's name. It is my belief that Cheryl visits Derrick to comfort him and to remind him of her love. He is a sweet and precious boy, and we all love him very much. Derrick loves Daniel incredibly. Whenever they hung out and spent time together, they had fun and were always loving of each other. I look at pictures of the three boys together—the pictures are so touching and show the love they have for each other. It warms my heart and brings a smile to my face. Derrick loves Robin very much— she helped raise him. He always loved to go up to Robin and lay his head on her shoulder. Derrick's unconditional love for Robin is strong. I am grateful to her for always being there to look out for and love Derrick the way she did. With his mom on the other side of the veil, Robin did her best to fill the void left by Cheryl's passing, and she did it wonderfully. Derrick's incredible capacity for unconditional love was a big help to me, as I went through these tough times. It was truly inspiring.

Samuel, as I wrote earlier, is our youngest son, and he was only two years old when his mom, Cheryl, passed away. He doesn't remember his mom because he was so young when she died. Samuel loves his mom very much and looks forward to being with her once again. I can imagine how much Cheryl looks forward to their reunion. Robin is the only mother that he knows; she was the mom who raised him along with me. Samuel, or "Sammers," as Robin liked to call him, loves her very much. They became very close before she returned to her heavenly home. When Robin got very sick in 2018, Samuel helped me care for her. He assisted me in taking her to her dialysis treatments, along with anything else that she needed assistance with, especially when I was not at home. One of the "scariest" was helping Robin come out of insulin shock when her blood sugar had gotten too low. This was no easy task at all, particularly when she was not very responsive to our assistance.

That year took a big toll on me and our family; I knew that I could always count on Samuel to assist Robin and me when dealing with her health. He was invaluable to us as her health steadily deteriorated. Samuel and Robin formed a strong bond from the beginning, from when they first met. He warmed to her immediately. When she came over to meet the boys for the first time, Samuel hopped over to her and asked her, "So are you going to marry my dad?" That really touched her, and their bond grew from that moment. Robin loves Samuel so very much, and they have become very close. Samuel loves his brother Daniel so much, and their bond as brothers is very strong. Daniel's passing hit Samuel very hard.

They spent many hours and even days playing video games together, as well as going out to lunch on Saturdays, watching movies and TV, and hanging out with each other and their friends. We have talked a lot about Daniel since his passing, about our memories of him, how he died, and what led up to his death. This helped me a lot while dealing with Daniel's loss. At times Samuel was the only person in whom Daniel would confide. Their love for each other is strong, and I am so grateful that they built such an incredible bond. They are brothers, and I am very proud of both of them.

When Robin passed away, Samuel was a great support to me. He would come up from his room to check to see how I was doing. He was concerned for me and how I was handling Robin's death. He knew how much I loved her and how much pain I was in. I am so grateful for him and for his looking out for me during this difficult time in our lives. Samuel still calls me to see how I am. He was incredibly supportive to me during my darkest hours, during my mourning for my beloved wives and son, and he still is. I am incredibly grateful for Samuel's continual love and support for me.

I love my boys with all my heart and am so proud and honored to be their father.

Elizabeth, our only daughter, was born to Robin and me three months prematurely. She spent four and a half months in the Utah Valley Medical Center NICU. She is our wonderful miracle. Elizabeth is so close to Robin, and the love that they share is strong. When Robin passed away, Elizabeth really handled her death better than I did. During the week after she died, I asked Elizabeth how she was and if she missed her mom. She told me that she did miss her mom, but that her mom was okay, and was no longer in pain, she was happy, and she loved us. Very simple and profound was her response. I took her to a counselor to talk about losing her mom. After a few sessions, the counselor said that Elizabeth was handling her mom's death well. Elizabeth looked at it in a straightforward way— her mom no longer suffered from her health issues, and Robin was . . . good. She missed her mom most definitely, but she was glad that Robin was no longer in pain. Elizabeth's example was such an inspiration for me. Her warmth and concern for me after her mom's death were comforting and touching.

She also would come and check on me and see how I was doing. Elizabeth has never been a real hugger, but when she felt that I was down or struggling, she would come up, give me a hug, and tell me that she loved me. This helped me a lot. She has such a sweet spirit, and I am so grateful for her and the time she took to connect with me when she knew I needed it. It is also great that the older she gets, the more of Robin I see in her—her looks and her mannerisms, etc. She is her mom's daughter.

She is my little girl and will always be. Elizabeth and Daniel were never very close. They never totally connected as she has with Samuel and Derrick. I know that she loves him, and when he passed, she was a big assistance to Robin in particular. Her innocence and her beautiful heart helped Robin and me after Daniel died. The caring and love that she showed us was beautiful, and we were very grateful for this "childlike love" that she showed for her parents. Elizabeth is very close to Samuel, and I am very grateful for this. I love my daughter very, very much, and it is an honor and a privilege to be her father.

It is with humility and gratitude that I have Derrick, Samuel, and Elizabeth still with me here in this mortal existence. We indeed never know what life will bring us next. I will love and cherish them every day and always. We never know on any given day what can 'happen. I implore you to do the same. Love and cherish your children, embrace them tightly, and revel in them. Honor your deceased loved one. Cherish your loved ones who remain here with you on earth, for we never know because life can kick us in the butt at any time.

My parents, siblings, and extended family, who were, and are, a great source of comfort, support, and strength for me and our kids. My mom and dad always stepped up to assist me with whatever I needed and helped me with taking care of the boys, especially when the boys were young. Mom and Dad were always there providing incredible support and strength for me and my family during our darkest hours. My dad provided valuable counsel and strength for me, as he always has. My mom was there with much-needed humor and support that only a mom can give to her child when they are in pain. To say that my parents were of great help to me during this time when I needed them most, is an incredible understatement. They were and are always there for me and my family when our need is great. For this, I am eternally grateful.

My oldest brother, Rob, his wife, Connie, and their daughter Erin traveled from Texas to give us support and love. This was awesome, and I will always appreciate them doing this for me and my family. I remember that Rob gave me wise and needed counsel when I was grieving. My brothers Ryan and Darin (Dude), my sister, Lynette, and my sisters-in-law Michelle and Kim, along with my brother-in-law, Dave, were a great help to me with wise counsel and support, always dropping everything to come to our aid and give us the support we needed. The day that Daniel suddenly passed away, Ryan was a great help to me and informed the family, including my parents, that Daniel had died. I am so grateful to Ryan for doing this. That, as you can imagine, was not an easy task. My brother-in-law, Dave, is like another brother to me, always there to assist me, whether it is to fix something in our house or to be willing to listen and provide good advice.

After Robin passed away, my sister, Lynette, and my sisters-in-law, Michelle, and Kim, took our daughter, Elizabeth, under their wings, and helped me greatly with her while I prepared for Robin's funeral, and to this day are a great support for her. I hope they know how much that means to me and that I will be eternally grateful. You see, Elizabeth had just lost her mom, and they were incredible with her. Elizabeth is profoundly hearing impaired. After Robin died, Elizabeth, my two sons, and several of my family members took sign language classes so that we could communicate better with Elizabeth. This was touching and incredibly supportive of my family to do this. I am so grateful to them for this showing of love and support for Elizabeth, especially since she had just lost her mom. And yes, Ryan and I had fun learning slang words in sign language.

My entire family showed up HUGE for me as I was dealing with my grief. My family was there for me and our children during the time when I was completely overwhelmed and hurting. I remember days when I was in so much pain and tired from sleepless nights. The sadness that I experienced from my loss was so overwhelming.

During this most difficult time, my family stepped up with open arms, unconditional love, and understanding hearts. The compassion and patience that they showed to me while I was in such pain were wonderful. Thank you all for being there for me and my family in our time of need, during our most difficult days. I am indeed eternally grateful to each and every one of you, for I am truly blessed to have been born into such a strong and loving family.

I am certain there are some of you who can understand and relate to what I am saying. This was a very difficult time for me, with so much to be taken care of within the first week after each of their passing. And when you are hurting and going through the most difficult thing anybody can go through in this lifetime, family support is invaluable.

Robin's family also showed up in a big way after her passing. They traveled from various parts of the country to attend her funeral and to give me and our children strength, support, and love. That was a huge showing of love and devotion for Robin, and I was deeply touched. My sister-in-law provided all the family pictures of Robin growing up, and others for the funeral collage to be displayed for her viewing and memorial service. I am incredibly thankful to Robin's mom and her family for their love and support.

Throughout all the losses I've experienced in my life, with the loss of my two beautiful wives, and my wonderful son, along with the fact that I've also lost some good friends. I have come to realize without a doubt, and to a whole new depth, the undeniable importance of family. Again, to me, it all starts with family. Family is everything.

I am sure many of you who are reading this book can completely understand and appreciate what I am saying. We— those of us who have experienced such loss—can rely on family for our support, comfort, and strength, when we experience such agonizing pain and sorrow following the loss of a loved one. If any of you, my readers, are finding it difficult to reach out to your family, I would urge and hope that you will. It will bring comfort to your heart to have the assurance that *you are not walking this path alone*. Family can be an incredible support system for you. It is my experience that you will be grateful that you reached out to them. They can provide you with valuable support and love, as you work through your grief.

> *Family is of infinite value. They are here to assist our Heavenly Father in his work of bearing us up through our most difficult and painful days. They are a godsend.*
> —*Lloyd C. Davis*

I have a friend who has lost both of his parents. Here is his story that he has shared with me to include in this book. Thank you, Michael, for allowing me to share your story with my readers.

Michael's Story

On November 11, 2012, my father passed away. He was eighty-two at the time and was living in a convalescent home near my brother and his family in Silverdale, Washington. Based on my visits there, it was a decent home, but my dad always spoke of going home. That was one of the more heart-tugging issues with Dad. We knew he didn't like being in the convalescent home, yet at 400-plus pounds, with signs of dementia and unable to walk, he required twenty-four-hour care as well as medical care nearby. My dad had several bladder infections over the course of the previous year. Each recurring infection rendered him more and more resistant to the antibiotics he was given, and with each passing occurrence, we were informed by the doctors that the next one could be the last.

As my dad was suffering from the infection that eventually took his life, we were preparing for the worst, as we had done with the prior infections. If you have ever been through this cycle, you may have experienced similar emotions. Hoping for the best, yet wondering what is "the best"? Knowing that my dad is waking up every day in a place he doesn't want to be, and knowing this is where he is going to be for the rest of his life, be it ten days or ten years, what is "the best"? Mom had passed fifteen years earlier. He missed her every day and wanted to be with her yet also wanted to be with us. So, the answer to the question of "what is the best?" is, I don't know. I was house-sitting for my sister-in-law the night my dad passed. I had left my phone in the kitchen, so I didn't hear it ring during the night. When I awoke and picked up my phone, I saw that I had about ten messages from my brother. I knew what they were before I listened but listened anyway.

In a way, my dad's passing was a relief. My mom, on the other hand, was a different story. She was sixty-four, and she and Dad had great plans for the rest of her life. Then one day the diagnosis of cancer came, and she was given a year to live. She passed two weeks after the diagnosis. Her death caught us by surprise. But Dad's was not a surprise. We knew it was coming, but not when. Dad wasn't really Dad anymore. The dad who used to ride us on his shoulders, play football out in the street with the neighbor kids, coach little league—the good dad, husband, and dedicated police officer was long gone. We would get small glimpses of that dad through sharing of memories, but his memory got fuzzy, and we saw the dad we once knew less and less. I had told my dad I loved him many times before he passed. I had no regrets. We bought him a casket with a silk-screen police emblem silk-screened on the lining. Not for him of course. But as a reminder of who he was . . . as one last memory for us.

How did I move on? Clear on who he was. Clear that I left nothing out that I would regret, and clear that this is part of a life cycle we all agreed to when we came here. There were some emotions, of course. The funeral and speaking were tough for me. Wheeling his casket out of the mortuary and into the hearse. The motorcycle police escort was very touching. Placing his casket on the gravesite where his body would rest with Mom was very healing.

How do we move on? We allow ourselves to grieve for the time it takes to grieve and accept what is. For some, it is shorter than it is for others. In this case, it was made somewhat easier in that we knew it was coming, and Dad who I knew as Dad had been gone for a while. I still miss him, as I do Mom, but the grieving part is long past, and life goes on. Our choice is to deny what is and live in the past, or accept what is and move on, just as life moves on.

Friends

Friends are angels who lift us to our feet when our
wings have trouble remembering how to fly.
—*Lorraine K. Mitchell*

In life one of our greatest achievements can be to obtain good friends. The type of friends that you can always rely on when the occasion calls for it, when you are in need. While writing my book I have made a lot of new friends, and I appreciate all their support. I am blessed to have a lot of good friends in my life, and for them, I am grateful.

I have two good friends, Tony, and Neal, as well as my grandma Eva, or as I call her, "Eva Chick," who have all passed away: along with my father-in-law John. I still go and visit and decorate their graves every Memorial Day in remembrance of them. It is my honor that I am still able to do this, especially with my kids.

My family adopted Grandma Eva while I was in high school. She became a great friend and support for my mom and our family. On Halloween, her home was a cherished destination where we loved to take our kids for trick-or-treating. We all love Eva Chick; she is a part of our family.

My late wife Robin's dad, John, became a friend as well as my father-in-law; he is a very good man, and Robin thought the world of him. I have never met a man who loved kids more than Grandpa John. My late friends Tony and Neal are very special to me, and they will always have an important place in my heart. Neal's stories and jokes were always a sense of fun and fascination for my boys on Thanksgiving.

Great friends in this life are golden. I have two friends in particular who were an incredible support for me and my family during those most difficult days—friends who helped lighten the load. After Daniel died, they remained on the scene with his body until the coroner came to receive him. You see, my family and I went up to my parent's house to be together on that terrible day. My wonderful friends also made sure that the coroner treated Daniel with care and respect as they took him away. These two friends are gold and very special to me, and they were a huge assistance to me while I was grieving after my losses. They are my lifelong childhood friends Lily and Rick. They have always been there for me in my time of need. No matter the time or the situation, they are always there to provide me with support and comfort.

I know that things happen for a reason, but what that reason is, we don't always know or understand. But this I do know—it is no accident that I am friends with Lil and Rick, and I know that we will always be friends. They provided me with incredible and invaluable support when I lost each of my loved ones. They are friends who love me unconditionally, and who dropped everything to come to my aid, with no questions asked. They knew that I needed them, and they came. And they continue to do so. For this, I am incredibly grateful, and I love them very much.

I have many other friends who have assisted me a lot during my journey—way too many to name in this book. Each and every one of them is of great value to me as well, and I love them all.

I really hope that all of you who are reading this book have close friends that you feel the same about. Friends who stand by you no matter what. Friends such as these will look out for you and come to your aid in those dark hours, in those dark days—those times when you are up against the wall because of the pain and intensity of your grief after the loss of your loved one. They can soothe your pain and ease your mind. These wonderful friends are God's gift to you.

Remember that when you are in moments of despair, these angels, your friends, can assist you and provide you with the comfort and strength that you need so very much. If you are in need, please reach out to them. You will be grateful that you did. It is my experience that such friends are a godsend, for with them, *you never have to walk this journey alone.*

Family and friends are our earthly guardian angels.

Friends are the angels who believe in us when we
have forgotten how to believe in ourselves.
—Anonymous

CHAPTER 11

Divine Connections

Miracles from God and Messages from Our Loved Ones

*Miracles happen every day. Not just in remote
country villages or at holy shrines halfway
across the globe, but here, in our own lives.*
—*Deepak Chopra*

Miracles happen. It is my experience that miracles are real and
are happening around us. They unfold not only in our own
lives but also in the lives of those around us. Sometimes people
tend to think that miracles only happen to others and not to
themselves or within their own lives. It is my feeling that some
miracles happen, and we don't even realize it.

It's like in the movie, *Miracles from Heaven*. One of the
daughters of the family that was depicted in the movie was
suffering from an incurable illness. During her treatment and
many hospital visits, there were many miracles that happened.
One miracle saved their daughter's life—an incredible miracle

that could not be explained by medicine. If you have seen the movie, then you know. In the movie, there were also less noticeable miracles that, at the time, the family didn't really know about or realize were happening. During the last part of the movie, when the mother spoke at a church service, she talked about the miracles in their lives that happened during this incredible ordeal that their family was going through. The miracles were beautiful acts of kindness from people they didn't even know, and at the time the family didn't realize that these selfless acts of kindness were happening. It was a wonderful, touching message. Miracles can come in the form of service from others, from their kindness, and from love.

In this chapter, I want to share with you two of my own stories as well as stories from others who have so generously shared them with me to be included in this book—stories of miracles and messages from our deceased loved ones, stories of the love that we share with our loved ones who have returned to their heavenly home.

Robin's and My Story

My amazing wife Robin became very ill in 2018.

While she was going into one of her dialysis treatments, she collapsed. Thankfully, my parents were taking her to her dialysis treatment that day. As she was walking into the dialysis center, she suddenly lost consciousness and as she was falling, my dad caught her. She was very fortunate that my dad was there helping her out of the car. My mom ran in—I tell you; she sprinted in and informed the dialysis clinic about Robin collapsing outside. They called for an ambulance, and Robin was taken to the ER.

We made many trips to the ER with Robin that year, and she spent a lot of 2018 either in the hospital or a physical rehabilitation center. I remember the daily visits to the Utah Valley Medical Center's ICU to visit her. Robin was diagnosed with several blood infections, including sepsis C-diff. Robin had sepsis three times that year. She flatlined several times while she was in the ER and in the ICU, and she was able to be brought back each time. This was most assuredly a scary, intense time in our lives. Robin had actually died in 2018, but by the grace of God, the doctors brought her back, and gratefully, she lived on.

Our Heavenly Father allowed her to return to us, and it was a blessing to have more time with her. He gave our family extra time with Robin before she finally returned to her heavenly home. This was a miracle for us and for our children, particularly for our daughter Elizabeth, because they were very close. The extra time with Robin, before she passed, gave us time to grow closer to our daughter. Robin was allowed to stay until she knew that we would be all right—all of us.

With loving grace, the Lord called her home to be with her dad and all her beloved ones on the other side. That was a miracle for me and my family. Through his benevolence, Heavenly Father blessed us with more time with my late wife Robin to make sure that we would be ok. For this, I will be eternally grateful.

Caroline's Story

I lost my husband suddenly to a heart attack on April 6, 2022. He died before I could get him to the hospital. We had discussed death and dying many times over the years and had promised each other that if it were possible, we would find a way to let each other know we were okay after we died.

The night of his death, I was lying in bed in shock and grief and was thinking about everything that had happened when I heard a rattling sound coming from the wardrobe. It sounded like my husband was hanging up his clothes as he did every night before bed. The door of the wardrobe was shut. We don't have a cat or anything that could have gotten inside it. I said aloud, "Alex! What are you doing in the wardrobe? I know you are okay. Thank you." The rattling of the hangers stopped then.

I cried buckets knowing that he had fulfilled his promise to let me know he was okay and that he was in the room with me. He had chosen to do something that sounded very normal and wasn't scary.

Joyce's Story

My daughter had spinal meningitis when she was five. My father-in-law was in a different hospital at the same time. We didn't tell him that my daughter was sick. They both came home, and my daughter told Grandpa that she was very sick, and he didn't go see her. He said, "I know you were sick," and my husband asked him how he knew. He said an angel came and told him it was time to come home. At the same time, he saw my daughter walk by his room, and she said, "Grandpa, I need you." He told the angel he couldn't go yet because his family needed him. What a wonderful miracle.

Sean's Story

I lost Rhonda on August 18, 2022. I was really hurting and riding a roller coaster of emotion after that until early January. My church doesn't hold evening services, but in January our pastor held an old-school style prayer meeting on each Sunday night. On the first one, I went up and prayed while crying and asking the Lord for help. That night while asleep, God, as only He can do, allowed Rhonda to talk to me. We were married for twenty-three years, so I know her voice. She told me, "Sean, I'm okay. You know where I'm at. Now I need you to live your life." Ever since then, I've been a lot more at ease. I still ride the roller coaster some, but it's nowhere as intense at times, and I have posted some of those on social media since January. But it gave me peace to hear her voice again and know that she is with the Lord, and I will see her again. That is my miracle.

In the last fourteen months, I lost my wife on August 18, 2022; my mom on July 13, 2022; my dad on December 2, 2022; and my sister on September 8, 2023. I have had it hard. Job had it harder than I do, but realize this: from the moment of Adam's first breath at creation, until the last person on earth takes their last breath and eternity begins, no one has ever had it as hard as Christ. He took the weight of every person's sin throughout history and took the punishment for one reason: He loves us and doesn't want us to suffer that punishment. Just tell Him you believe He saved you by dying and rising again.

Cindee's Story

Bryce passed away on January 18, 2023. Two weeks before he passed away, we found out that he had metastatic cancer. As we talked about what was going to happen and made plans, he commented that he was okay with dying—he just didn't want to leave me. We had just celebrated four years of marriage and had finally found joy after so many years of being alone after divorce. We had been sealed the year before and knew that this would be a short moment and I would be placed in my Heavenly Father's care. When he took his final breath, I laid my head down on his hand and cried. His children, brother, and my daughter were with me. I felt Bryce behind me with his hand on my shoulder. He said, "I don't want to leave you." I felt the spirits of his family waiting for him. I told him he needed to go. I had to focus on what was happening in mortality, and he needed to go to his family. I told them I would be okay and that I loved him. I felt him leave, and I could feel the joy of those who welcomed him home. I know the veil has opened many times since his death, and I have felt his love, reassurance, and humor.

Marilyn's Story

My "tender mercies"

In 2010 my husband, Brant, was in a catastrophic accident where he broke twenty-three bones, including six vertebrae, and had a basal skull fracture. Amazingly he was able to fight back from his injuries and return to an almost normal life, but only a year later a massive blood clot blocked the main artery to his bowels, and they were not able to save him. They came out during the last surgery and told me there was no possible way he could live. We made the decision to let family and friends come to say goodbye, and then we would turn off his life support. My only daughter was sixteen and extremely close to her dad. She was one of the last ones to go into his room to say goodbye. I stood in the hallway, but I could hear her speaking to him.

Through her sobs, she told him how badly she needed him and that he was supposed to be there to watch her graduate, get married, have babies, etc. She was completely distraught, and I was not able to comfort her. She decided to go home with my sister rather than stay when we turned off life support.

When I entered his room after she left, there was an absolutely terrible feeling of grief. I was very sure that, even with being sedated, my husband had heard her say goodbye and he was feeling just as distraught as she was. He would have done anything to stay with his little girl. I asked my father-in-law to give him a blessing and let him know that it was okay to go and that we would rally around and take care of each other.

As soon as the blessing ended that awful sense of grief that had been in the room was gone, and a quiet sense of peace replaced it. I have no doubt at all that his spirit left his body at that point. They had warned me that when we turned off life support it might take a few minutes while he tried to breathe on his own, but that did not happen at all. He was no longer in that broken body.

I didn't tell my daughter about it for several years, fearing that would make things harder for her. Several years later when I did tell her she wept—but she was weeping from joy. It meant so much to her to know that her dad had heard her and didn't want to leave her. Of course, we had wished for a different kind of miracle, one that would have had him stay, but it was still a miracle for us to see the power of love and the power of a priesthood blessing.

My second experience happened about six months after Brant died. My youngest son, who was twenty years old and not active in the church, went with me to his grandparents' house to help them move furniture. His cousin's husband and four-year-old son were there as well. His little four-year-old cousin asked him, "Do you talk to your dad?" He answered gently, "No, Lee, my dad is dead." Then that sweet little four-year-old replied, "I know, but I talk to him all the time." He pointed his little finger heavenward and said with great seriousness, "He is there for you." What a beautiful little miracle to know that even though I do not have the gift to be able to sense my husband near me, he is there, and that sweet little boy could talk to him.

Renae's Story

A few days after my husband had passed, I was overwhelmed with the amount of money a casket would cost. DeWayne didn't want to be cremated, so I had to have a casket. There was no life insurance and no extra money. So, I decided to build the casket. I knew I would be capable of building it; however, I simply couldn't emotionally accomplish the task. On top of that, I really wanted one that reflected his personality. DeWayne was a cowboy at heart, and none of the caskets I'd seen even remotely seemed like one he would choose.

When DeWayne was alive, he was always asking our neighbor Larry to help him build something. Larry was always so busy that they never could get hooked up to do anything together. Being in the swirl I was, my mother decided to call Larry and ask for his assistance. This was during COVID as well. Timing for the funeral was critical, as the state had lifted some restrictions with a warning that the restrictions might be put back in place. We had a day and a half to build it!

Thankfully Larry agreed. He and I met to decide how and what to make it out of. I really wanted tongue and groove, but money was an issue. We decided on plywood with burned accents. Oh, how I wanted the tongue and groove! So, I prayed that if DeWayne wanted the tongue and groove, Larry would be able to get it at the right price.

Larry headed out the next morning to gather materials. He got the flat strap for strength in the bottom. He got the handles. He got the lumber. He got fasteners and metal accents. When I met with him at the wood shop, he came out the door expressing "a change of plans."

My heart sank. *What now?* I thought. Larry approached with his head down. He stepped up to me and then looked up with the biggest smile on his face. "You got what you wanted! Come and see!" When I went to the lumber yard, I told them I was building a casket and that we'd like tongue and groove. The guy said they had some remnants from an order. There was just enough, and since it was remnants, it was cheaper than the plywood!"

The sight of what he'd built just filled my soul with relief! It was beautiful. Larry went to work, and the next morning my sister and I went to meet him at the metal shop. Becky and I helped bend and shape and held while Larry welded and nailed accents. Then we loaded it to take home and do the interior. Silk sheets were used for the lining. I found some fake leaves to put around on the top of the inside. I felt like it still wasn't quite right. Knowing DeWayne loved horses, the picture he'd gotten from my sister at Christmas fit perfectly. And so, I put it inside the lid. Stepping back to get an overall view, I wondered, "DeWayne, what do you think?" Suddenly, a wash of warmth cascaded from the tip of my head, through my body all the way to my toes. My heart swelled! "Yes, DeWayne it is beautiful." And it was.

Brittany's Story

My husband passed away on March 9th. He was only thirty-five. Together, we have two sons who are five and nine. My five-year-old son has had nightmares every single night since his passing. About a week ago, he woke up from a nap and immediately came to me to tell me he saw Daddy in his dream. This is how he described the dream:

"I saw a monster like I always do in my dreams. I was so scared. And then the monster turned into Jesus. Jesus told me not to be afraid. That monsters are not real. Then I saw Daddy standing next to Jesus. He gave me a sucker for being such a good boy. Then he gave me a family crest coin and told me to protect Mommy and my family. Everything was golden—even the clouds were gold. It was so beautiful." He has not had a nightmare since that dream!

Debi's Story

Our miracle:

My husband had recently been diagnosed with cancer and had to go to Lubbock for radiation treatment. Lubbock is two and a half hours from us, so my husband was going to stay in housing provided free of charge to cancer patients undergoing treatment. He met a very nice lady with whom he spoke daily when she came in for some routine procedures in her treatment. We were about to lose our car due to loss of income. Well, they got to talking about the car possibly going to be towed for nonpayment. She offered to pay off the car. She got the info from my husband, and she paid off the car for $18,000. A week later she died from her disease.

We also had a delivery of two air conditioners to be installed by my church that month. We had not complained about being overheated, but it was mentioned in church, and right away they helped us out with some air conditioning. We were also gifted with some travel money for his trips to Lubbock. Also, we had been having lunch together at a truck stop during one of his visits and someone paid for our meal. The reason? We were NOT talking or looking at our phones. We had so many miracles during those months; it was incredible!

Cheryl's and my story

After my late wife Cheryl passed away, I was in pain and scared. I didn't really know what I was going to do next. I mean, raising three boys alone. The things that had taken place before Cheryl passed away. We were divorced, but we were, and have, reconciled our relationship. We love each other very much, eternally. But when she passed away it was a jolt of incredible pain to me. Having just lost Cheryl, as well as raising and taking care of the boys, I was very confused and feeling overwhelmed.

The night following Cheryl's funeral, I was confused and in pain. It was excruciating. I felt like I was on the edge of an abyss. So that night I was lying on my bed with tears in my eyes, from the time I spent in emotional contemplation that evening.

It was then that I suddenly felt a surge of energy rushing through my body, it felt like this energy filled my every cell. This energy surrounded me, and I felt as if I was going to be lifted off the bed. Such an intense and warm energy flowed through me. As this was happening to me, I realized that it was my wife Cheryl comforting me. The "heavenly energy" that I was feeling became warm and calming to me. I then heard

Cheryl whisper into my ear that she was okay and free of the torment. She told me that she loved me and the boys, and that she would be with us always, watching over us. I felt her kiss me on the cheek before she returned to her heavenly home. I became very calm and serene, as I fell into a peaceful asleep. I will never forget this experience that I shared with her, from the minute that I felt the energy surge until she left to return home. Well, it was wonderful.

Miracles can come forth as answers to prayers. They can be unmistakably visible or quiet and subtle. Whether they are big and easily seen or unheralded and not noticed by us at the time, miracles can change lives and bring us closer to our Creator.

Miracles are those whispers, feelings, and communications of love and comfort from our loved ones who have passed away. It is my humble belief that miracles come to us as gifts from our Heavenly Father. Miracles do happen. They are real. They are humbling. They are beautiful. They are divine.

The bonds we share transcend life and
death. In the realm beyond, I send you
messages of love and comfort, forever.
—Unknown

CHAPTER 12

Epilogue

You Will Never Walk Alone

He whispered, "My precious child,
I love you and will never leave you.
Never, ever, during your trials and testing.
When you saw only one set of footprints,
It was then that I carried you."
—From the poem "Footprints in the Sand"

Each of us has a unique way of responding to the loss of our loved ones. No two individuals grieve in the same manner, as we all possess our own distinct identities. Remember that no one else should determine how you grieve. The process of grieving is personal and varies for each person, reflecting our individuality. I feel it is important to state again, that grief is not one size fits all. It is not the same for everyone. You need to be able to grieve in a way that works for you—how it will best serve you. To grieve in your own way. The best advice I can give is to be true to yourself and to your feelings. Trust yourself and listen to your spirit. "Getting out of your head" and listening to your heart can give you such clarity. It is also very important to remember that **you will never walk alone**. Your loved ones will always be with you, giving you comfort and support. As is our Heavenly Father—He is always there for us to give us comfort, guidance, and strength.

I have written about steps that assisted me on my journey toward healing and peace. These steps and actions that I took assisted me greatly in finding the healing that I so desperately needed, and they aided me in achieving something that I never thought possible: peace.

I wrote about these steps: accepting and embracing our emotions; placing our loved ones in a sacred and honored place in our hearts where we will always have them with us; and creating a virtual memorial for each of my loved ones who passed away. Writing a tribute to your loved ones is so impactful, along with choosing pictures and music to go with your words of love. This can be like an obituary for sure. Through a virtual memorial, you have the opportunity to continue to write affectionate messages in their memory and incorporate additional photos and music. I would invite you to create a virtual memorial website for your deceased loved ones. It is a beautiful way to honor them with your love.

Another step included sharing my feelings, experiences, and stories with others in various ways. I found this to be cathartic and very healing indeed. It is my hope that you do as well.

I also chose to move forward in a positive way, the path of light and love. Recognizing that anger and indifference are not the true pathways forward to healing and peace. Through love and forgiveness, you can find strength and solace.

The spiritual part of my journey toward healing was vital to me. My knowledge that we will once again be reunited with our loved ones who have passed gives me incredible joy and comfort. It is my prayer that you can find this as well. May you be able to find comfort and strength in your spiritual journey while you navigate your own path through your grief and moving forward.

As I navigated through my grief, my Heavenly Father was with me the entire way, and He still is. It is my profound belief that as we navigate our own journey, He will always be at our side— for we are His children, and He is always there for us.

In writing this book, I also shared about finding a place to go where I could be alone: a sanctuary or place of refuge where I could be one with my thoughts and my feelings. That is very helpful to me. A place where I could listen to music and center myself. To recharge my batteries. It might help you to find a place where you can be alone to meditate and center yourself. To be with your thoughts and feelings, while searching for balance as you navigate your own path, toward the healing that you desire so much. It is my feeling that this could possibly be a strengthening and awakening experience for you, as it was for me.

I have also shared about the importance of family, and the vital role that they played throughout my healing process, and the comfort and support that I received from them, as well as the support that I received from my friends. I pray that you have family and friends from whom you can find comfort and support after the passing of your loved one. I know that it can sometimes be difficult to reach out to our family and friends for assistance. But it is so worth it. The love, comfort, and support could be just at the other end of a phone call, text, or email. It is my humble experience that, as you travel your journey of working through your grief, **you will never walk alone.**

Sharing Our Stories

I again want to emphasize how incredibly cathartic and healing it was for me to share my story with others. Believe me when I say, that not only does it bring profound comfort to us when we open up and share our experiences, but it also aids those who are kind enough to listen.

I encourage you to consider sharing the story of your loss with others, it can ease the pain that has scarred your heart. When people inquire, it is because they genuinely care and want to provide support during this challenging time—and sometimes it feels good to just "talk it out." You can choose to share your thoughts and emotions through social media or any other medium that feels comfortable to you. By allowing others to read about your deep affection and how you honor the memory of your departed loved one, you offer them the opportunity to bear witness to your journey of healing and remembrance.

When I lost my son, Daniel, I wanted to bear witness to the world about how honorable and wonderful his life was and how great a man he is. I felt a divine need to do this. Perhaps you, too, share a similar sentiment regarding the loved one you have lost. If so, remember that the world stands ready to offer you a platform to honor their memory. At times, amid the immense grief that engulfs you, you might find yourself grappling with the belief that your words may seem redundant or repetitive. I feel this myself at times. In this, I would just say follow your heart.

Throughout this book, I have shared with you what has helped me in working through my grief, and I have given examples of the processes and steps that I have taken along the way. When you are on your own journey to work through your grief, you should do what works for you. Embark on your own path toward healing and ultimately peace. Getting out of your mind and feel—listen to your heart. Get in touch with the love that you and your deceased loved one share. The love and devotion that you have for them can be the driving force behind your journey. Supported by your departed loved ones, you can work through your grief and eventually come to a place where you are at peace.

Finding peace begins with knowing that our deceased loved ones reside within the embrace of their Creator and that we will be with them once again. Along with the knowledge that when our time comes to return home, they will be there waiting for us with open arms and tears of joy at that wonderful reunion. Understanding that you can honor them and show your love for them while you are moving forward, can put your heart at ease.

When we have found that joyous healing that we were in search of, and we are truly at peace, we feel comfort and a calming clarity that we have worked through our grief with love and with a forgiving heart, and knowing that we have trusted ourselves, and have followed our hearts throughout our journey. It's finding the courage and strength to move forward; accepting that life must go on, while remembering and honoring the lives that we shared with our loved ones who have passed away. This is what it feels like to be at peace with your grief—to have found healing, and where we are aligned intellectually, spiritually, and emotionally, regarding our grief, where we have discovered profound contentment as we navigate life's path.

This is what I mean by finally finding healing and being at peace. It is where feelings about your loss and the love that you have for your deceased loved ones are aligned. Your heart is healed. You think about and feel your loved ones, and you have clarity as well as calmness in your spirit regarding them. There is no anger or guilt. This is wonderful; this is a warm feeling of serenity. We can all obtain this; we can create this. My humble belief, and what I learned through my experiences is that you can create a sense of tranquility when it comes to mourning the loss of your departed loved one.

Yes, we can still be sad because of our separation. We **will** be sad sometimes. I totally understand how that feels—the feeling of being sad because they're not with me anymore here on earth. Our sadness and longing to be with them will turn to loving memories and the warm anticipation of being with our deceased loved ones again. Because your heart has mended and you have found the solace you so desired, you can discover a calming peace. You can have the clarity and the peace of mind and of spirit that warms your heart. Your grief is no longer a burden but a blessing. I am there—I am at peace with my grief. It is my wish that you can be at peace with your grief as well and that you will find healing.

The path can be tough—it is hard work, digging deep, and deciding that we are willing to do what it takes to get there. Wow, yeah, there are times when I found it easier to lie to myself. To lie to others. If that's how you feel sometimes, well, you're not alone; I've been there. I completely understand. To find true healing—to heal our broken hearts—requires that we be truly honest with ourselves. It requires us to be humble and to be real with ourselves. At times that is not fun or comfortable. But neither is being stuck in our grief.

Wherever you are in the process of dealing with your grief, acknowledge it—feel it. Use your emotions and feelings to navigate through your journey. Use inspiration and love to guide you.

Unconditional love is the only way forward to find healing and peace. Use the pure love that you have for your deceased loved one to aid you. To be your bright light when things seem dark. Let their love for you be your *beacon*. Letting your love for them and your desire to be an eternal family be your driving force to find forgiveness, healing, and peace.

By embracing the process of self-discovery and embarking on your personal voyage toward healing, you can unlock profound transformation. Connect with the core motivations that drive your need and aspiration to progress beyond grief's grasp. Seek out the guiding light, your *beacon*, that holds immense significance and serves as your wellspring of inspiration on this healing path. Embrace unwavering honesty within, entrusting yourself to the benevolence and divine support of your higher power. In this profound journey, trust in your own instincts and remain authentic to your true self. Trust yourself.

As I wrote earlier in this book, while dealing with my grief, and the profound anguish that I was experiencing, I never questioned or lost my faith; I trusted my Heavenly Father as I navigated that difficult path to find healing and peace. That is my bottom line of this book.

It is my sincere hope that you can do this as well—Please trust God, for he will always be there as you travel your journey to healing.

And always remember that
you will never walk this path alone.

When you feel you are comfortable enough and are ready to share your own story of healing with others, I invite you to *pay it forward*. To share your story about your journey with others. And then ask them to do the same—to pay it forward as well. It is my hope that together we can create a huge ripple effect of healing for those who have lost a loved one.

With humility and much gratitude, I am honored, and I thank you for giving me the opportunity of sharing with you the story of my journey toward finding healing and peace, after the loss of my loved ones. I love them with all my heart. Again, it is my hope that you, too, can find healing and peace as well, and I ask God to watch over you and your family during this trying time. And finally, may God watch over and bless all those who are suffering and in pain from the loss of a loved one.

Have not I commanded thee? Be strong and of a good
courage; be not afraid, neither be thou dismayed: for
the Lord thy God is with thee whithersoever thou goest.
—Joshua 1:9

This is the conclusion of **this book.**But
my story continues . . .

ACKNOWLEDGMENTS

To my departed loved ones: my wife Cheryl, my wife Robin, and my son Daniel. You are all the inspiration for this book. Thank you for the lessons you taught me, and for the growth that we experienced together. Your continued support for me throughout the process of writing this book, has been comforting and strengthening. Your lives touched me beyond measure, and your love and influence have assisted me and becoming who I am today. I thank God every day for the blessings of having you in my life, and of us all being together as a family for eternity. I will always remember, miss, and love you all, for you are always in my heart.

To my three children who remain with me on the earth: Derrick, Samuel, and Elizabeth. You are an absolute joy to me. You always look out for your old dad. I will always appreciate your concern and love for me. You are what I have left of our small family in this earthly existence. I am very proud of each and every one of you. I am grateful for your strength and perseverance as you have traveled this journey alongside me, for I know that this has been very difficult for you as well. I will always be grateful and cherish all three of you. One of the greatest blessings God has given me is that of being your father. I love you all very much.

To my parents for all the incredible support and comfort that you give to me and my family. You are always there when we need you. For my dad for always giving us such a stalwart and strong example of faith, throughout our lives. For my mom, who told me to "stay the course" while I was writing this book. Mom, I am so very grateful for these wise, inspired words; for your believing in me, and for the undying support that you and Dad have given me throughout my journey of bringing this book to reality. Thank you for always being there for me during my most difficult days and trials. Mom, thank you for passing to me the gift of expressing myself through the written word. I am grateful that our Heavenly Father has blessed me with such loving and supportive parents.

To my siblings and their spouses. You will always have our undying gratitude for the comfort, strength, and love that you gave us when we needed it most, for showing up HUGE for me and my family, for always having my back, and for always being a source of incredible support for me and my family. I am truly blessed and grateful for you all.

To my extended family and friends who always give us words of encouragement, support, and love. For always being there for me and my family and showing up to provide help even when we thought we didn't need it. You are always a big example to me. Your kindness and love will always be with me and my family.

To my late wife Robin's mom Orilla, and her family for the support, comfort, and love that you give to me and our children, and for welcoming us into your family with open arms and open hearts. Our kids really love you. So much so that my late son, Daniel, changed his middle name to John, after my late wife Robin's dad, to honor him. I thank you all for your continual support and friendship.

To my late son, Daniel's, place of employment for the words and acts of support that you gave willingly and selflessly. I am eternally grateful for how well you treated Daniel and for donating money for his funeral. He did love his job and his coworkers very much.

To the faculty, staff and my late son Daniel's fellow students at Stevens-Henager College in Orem, Utah. Thank you for your love, support and friendship to my son Daniel while he attended. He loved his time at this fine institution. Thanks for the kindness that you all showed him, and for honoring him with an honorary degree, that was given to me at your commencement ceremony after he passed away. I am grateful that he attended Stevens-Henager College and the many friends that he made there.

To my place of employment during this time in my life: I appreciate the time off work that you gave me to take care of all the arrangements and time to take care of my family and myself.

Thank you to all the many doctors, nurses, physical therapists, dialysis techs, and many healthcare staff who took care of my Robin, providing her with the wonderful care and professional service that she needed during her battle with her health. You were all great and we will always be grateful to you for your professionalism and your kindness.

Thank you to everyone who shared your beautiful stories with me to be included in this book. For being willing to share with my readers, your experiences, and the love that you share with your deceased loved ones.

Thank you to Self-Publishing School and Selfpublishing. com for all the assistance that you gave to me throughout my journey towards getting my book published. For assisting me in making this dream come true.

Thank you to the Selfpublishing.com community, along with my fellow authors who have been a great support and inspiration for me throughout our journey together.

Thank you to my editor, Staci Mauney. I appreciate your continued assistance and feedback to me while I was getting my manuscript ready for publication.

Thank you to my beta readers Lynne, Jim, and Kim for your time and very valuable feedback regarding my manuscript. You were a big help to me.

Thank you to my Heavenly Father and to our Savior for the continual inspiration, support, comfort, and strength that You always give me and my family. Thank you for the incredible patience that You have always shown to me. I could not have gone through this without you and the knowledge of the fact that we will be a family forever. For I know that I will be reunited with my loved ones again.

Finally, to our Lord and Savior Jesus Christ for the blessing of His resurrection, making it possible for us to live on after death, providing us the blessing of being with our loved ones for eternity.

Thank you to each and every one of you.

ABOUT THE AUTHOR

Lloyd grew up in Lehi, Utah. He is the son of Dr. Kent B. and Lois P. Davis—he has four siblings: Rob, Ryan, Lynette, and Darin (Dude).

He pursued his academic studies in psychology and political science at both Utah State University and Utah Valley University. Lloyd married his late wife Cheryl in 1984. They resided in Lehi and then American Fork, Utah, with their three boys, Derrick, Daniel, who is deceased, and Samuel. Lloyd again moved back to Lehi, Utah, after he married his second wife Robin in 1998, who has since passed away. They resided there with their children for twenty-one years.

Lloyd has been self-employed and is the original owner and founder of Royal Crown Dental Lab as well as the owner of All-American Deli and Republic Strategies. Lloyd has worked in sales, business management, and public affairs.

Lloyd has also been very involved in politics. He has worked with many political campaigns and has run for public office himself. He served as a state and county delegate as well as a voting precinct chair. Politics is one of Lloyd's great passions.

What is most important to Lloyd is his faith and family. Family gives him the most joy in life. He would rather spend time with his family than do anything else. Lloyd also loves Harley-Davidson motorcycles and going on road trips. He likes golf, listening to music, target shooting, photography, reading, and writing. It was after Lloyd's first wife, Cheryl, passed away that he decided he needed to write this book. His departed loved ones are the inspiration for it. It is Lloyd's passion and his purpose to have this book finally published. Writing this book has been a work of love. Lloyd's path of working through his grief and finding healing and peace has been a transformational journey of love, sweat, and tears.

If My Book Helped

Please Let Me Know by Leaving a Review of My Book.

Your feedback means a lot to me, and
I genuinely value your input.

I really look forward to your thoughts on my book.

Please take two minutes now to leave a helpful review on
Amazon letting me know what you thought of the book:

https://lloydcdavis.com/review

Thanks so much!
~Lloyd C. Davis

REFERENCES

1. Cheryl Davis virtual memorial, https://www.virtual-memorials.com/main. php?action=view&mem_id=323&page_no=1
2. Daniel Davis virtual memorial, https://virtual-memorials.com/main. php?action=view&mem_id=27484&page_no=1
3. Robin Davis virtual memorial, https://virtual-memorials.com/main. php?action=view&mem_id=28024&page_no=1
4. https://www.virtual-memorials.com/
5. Monarch of the Glenn, Season 1 episode 5

Lloyd C Davis

Author of:
Heartache to Healing
Navigating Grief and Finding Peace

Contact Information
Email: lloydc.davis@gmail.com
Website: https://www.lloydcdavis.com/